Fast Cash Flow

The AI-Enhanced Day Trader's Guide to Instant Wealth! - Smart Strategies for Rapid Gains

By

Ernie Braveboy

Table of Contents

The information herein is offered for informational purposes solely, and is universal as so. The presentation of the information is without contract or any type of guarantee assurance.

The trademarks that are used are without any consent, and the publication of the trademark is without permission or backing by the trademark owner. All trademarks and brands within this book are for clarifying purposes only and are the owned by the owners themselves, not affiliated with this document.

Table of Contents

Foreword

In the rapidly evolving world of finance, the intersection of artificial intelligence (AI) and day trading represents a frontier that is reshaping the very fabric of the markets. "Fast Cash Flow: The AI-Enhanced Day Trader's Guide to Instant Wealth! - Smart Strategies for Rapid Gains" is not just a book; it is a beacon for those ready to navigate this new terrain with confidence and acumen.

The genesis of this book lies in the recognition of a transformative shift in the trading landscape. As traditional barriers crumble under the weight of technological advancement, the democratization of financial markets has welcomed a new breed of traders. These individuals, armed with nothing more than a computer and an internet connection, are not just participating in the markets; they are poised to dominate them, thanks to AI.

This book is crafted for the aspirant who sees beyond the conventional wisdom of slow and steady wins the race. It is for the bold, the daring, and the quick-witted who understand that in the realm of day trading, time is not just money—it is everything. With AI as your ally, this book will guide you to make swift, informed decisions, capitalizing on opportunities that others might miss.

As you turn these pages, you will embark on a journey that begins with the foundational principles of day trading and AI. You will be equipped with the knowledge to set up your trading station, armed with the tools that enable you to not just participate but excel in the market. The strategies outlined here are designed to propel you from novice to expert, ensuring that you can navigate the volatile waters of day trading with the poise of a seasoned veteran.

However, this book is more than a mere guide to strategies and tools. It is a manifesto for risk management, a crucial aspect often overlooked by many in the heat of the moment. It is a testament to the power of ethical trading and a reminder that in the quest for rapid gains, integrity should never be compromised.

As you delve into the advanced techniques and the insights on the future of AI in day trading, remember that this book is not the end of your journey but the beginning. The world of AI-enhanced day trading is dynamic, and staying ahead requires continuous learning and adaptation.

To those who stand on the brink of this exciting new era, "Fast Cash Flow" offers not just strategies for financial success but a vision for a future where AI and human ingenuity converge to create unprecedented opportunities. The path to instant wealth and rapid gains is fraught with challenges, but with this book as your guide, you are well-equipped to turn those challenges into stepping stones for success.

Welcome to the future of day trading. Welcome to "Fast Cash Flow."

Acknowledgments

Writing "Fast Cash Flow: The AI-Enhanced Day Trader's Guide to Instant Wealth! - Smart Strategies for Rapid Gains" has been an exhilarating journey, one that could not have been embarked upon without the support and inspiration from a myriad of individuals and experiences that have shaped this endeavor.

First and foremost, my gratitude extends to the pioneers and innovators in the fields of Artificial Intelligence and financial technology. Their relentless pursuit of advancement and their willingness to push the boundaries of what is possible have not only inspired this book but have also transformed the landscape of day trading and finance as a whole.

Special thanks are owed to the trading community—both the seasoned veterans and the enthusiastic novices. The discussions, debates, and shared experiences within this vibrant community have been invaluable. Their insights and real-world experiences have greatly contributed to the practical approach of this book.

I am profoundly grateful to my family and friends for their unwavering support and encouragement. Their belief in my vision and their patience through the countless hours spent researching, writing, and revising have been the cornerstone of this project.

Acknowledgment must also be made to the academic and professional experts who generously shared their time and knowledge. Their rigorous review and constructive feedback have been instrumental in ensuring the accuracy and reliability of the content presented.

To my editor and the publishing team, your expertise and dedication have been pivotal in transforming a manuscript into a polished and accessible guide for traders around the world. Your attention to detail and commitment to excellence have been truly remarkable.

Lastly, but certainly not least, I extend my deepest appreciation to you, the reader. Your eagerness to learn, to adapt, and to embrace the new frontiers of day trading with AI is the ultimate inspiration for this book. This book is for you, and it is my sincere hope that it serves as a valuable tool in your journey to financial success.

Thank you all for being part of this journey. Here's to achieving rapid gains and unlocking the potential of AI-enhanced day trading together.

How to Use This Book

"Fast Cash Flow: The AI-Enhanced Day Trader's Guide to Instant Wealth! - Smart Strategies for Rapid Gains" is designed to be both a comprehensive guide and a practical toolkit for anyone looking to harness the power of AI in day trading. Whether you're a complete novice to the world of trading or an experienced trader keen on integrating AI into your strategies, this book is structured to facilitate a smooth and effective learning journey.

Start with the Basics

Even if you have some experience in day trading, I recommend starting from the beginning of the book. The initial chapters lay a foundational understanding of day trading and AI, crucial for grasping the more advanced concepts and strategies discussed later.

Progress at Your Own Pace

The chapters are structured to build upon each other, but feel free to move through the book at a pace that suits your learning style. If a particular section or concept is already familiar to you, it might be tempting to skip ahead. However, even experienced traders might find new insights in these sections, thanks to the unique perspective of applying AI in day trading.

Engage with Practical Exercises

Throughout the book, you'll encounter practical exercises and challenges. Engaging with these hands-on activities is vital for cementing your understanding of the concepts discussed and for gaining real-world skills in AI-enhanced day trading.

Use the Appendices

The appendices are rich resources for quick reference and further exploration. From the glossary of terms to recommended AI trading software and further reading, these sections are designed to support your ongoing learning and trading practice.

Stay Updated

The world of AI and day trading is fast-evolving. Use this book as a springboard to keep abreast of the latest trends, technologies, and strategies in the field. Join online forums, subscribe to relevant publications, and continue to educate yourself beyond the pages of this book.

Apply the Knowledge

Knowledge gains true value when applied. As you learn from this book, start applying the strategies and insights to your day trading practice. Begin with simulated trading environments if you're not ready to risk real capital, and gradually progress to live trading as you gain confidence.

Reflect and Adapt

Finally, take time to reflect on your progress and the outcomes of the strategies you implement. The most successful traders are those who continuously analyze their performance, learn from their experiences, and adapt their approaches based on both successes and setbacks.

"Fast Cash Flow" is more than just a book; it's your companion on the journey to achieving rapid gains through AI-enhanced day trading. Embrace the journey, apply the lessons, and transform your day trading endeavors into a successful venture.

Introduction

Welcome to "Fast Cash Flow: The AI-Enhanced Day Trader's Guide to Instant Wealth! - Smart Strategies for Rapid Gains." In this dynamic era where technology meets finance, the advent of Artificial Intelligence (AI) in the realm of day trading has opened doors to possibilities that were once deemed science fiction. This book is a testament to the transformative power of AI in the financial markets and a guide to harnessing this power for personal financial success.

The journey into day trading is often fraught with myths of instant riches and tales of dramatic losses. The truth, as you will discover, lies somewhere in between. It is a path that requires knowledge, discipline, strategy, and now more than ever, a keen understanding of technological advancements, particularly AI. The goal of this book is to demystify the process of using AI in day trading and to provide you with a clear, actionable strategy for leveraging these technologies to achieve rapid financial gains.

Day trading, by its very nature, is a fast-paced endeavor that demands quick decision-making and the ability to adapt to rapidly changing market conditions. The introduction of AI into this environment has not only enhanced the speed and efficiency with which traders can operate but has also provided unprecedented levels of market insight and analytical power. However, with great power comes great responsibility, and the effective use of AI in day trading requires more than just a superficial understanding of the technology.

This book is designed to take you from a foundational understanding of day trading and AI, through the nuts and bolts of setting up and implementing AI-enhanced trading strategies, to managing the risks and ethical considerations that come with these powerful tools. Whether you are new to the world of trading or an experienced trader looking to integrate AI into your strategies, this guide will provide you with the insights and tools you need to succeed.

As we embark on this journey together, remember that the ultimate goal is not just to achieve "fast cash flow" but to do so in a manner that is sustainable, ethical, and aligned with your personal financial goals. The world of AI-enhanced day trading is exciting, dynamic, and full of potential. With the right approach, discipline, and a willingness to learn, you can tap into this potential and transform your financial future.

Let's begin this journey together, and unlock the secrets to leveraging AI for day trading dominance and transforming insights into income.

Why AI in Day Trading?

The fusion of Artificial Intelligence (AI) with day trading is not just a trend; it's a paradigm shift that is redefining the landscape of financial markets. This integration addresses several core challenges and opportunities in day trading, making AI not just a useful tool but a revolutionary force in trading strategies.

Enhanced Decision-Making Speed

In the world of day trading, where markets fluctuate by the second, the speed of decision-making can make or break a trader's success. AI excels in processing vast amounts of data at speeds incomprehensible to the human mind. This capability allows traders to identify and act on opportunities much faster than ever before, providing a significant edge in a highly competitive environment.

Superior Data Analysis

Day trading relies heavily on the analysis of complex and often chaotic market data. AI, with its advanced algorithms and machine learning capabilities, can sift through this data, identify patterns, and predict market movements with a level of accuracy and depth that is beyond human analysis. This deep insight enables traders to make more informed decisions, reducing guesswork and enhancing the probability of success.

Emotionless Trading

One of the biggest challenges in day trading is managing emotions. Fear and greed can lead to irrational decisions, resulting in losses. AI, devoid of emotions, operates on logic and predefined parameters, ensuring that trading decisions are consistent and unbiased. This objectivity helps in maintaining a disciplined trading approach, crucial for long-term success.

Risk Management

AI systems can be programmed to recognize risky trading scenarios and automatically adjust strategies to minimize losses. This proactive approach to risk management is invaluable, especially in volatile markets where rapid responses are crucial. AI's ability to continually learn and adapt from market conditions and past trades further refines risk management strategies over time.

Accessibility and Efficiency

AI democratizes day trading by making sophisticated analysis and trading strategies accessible to a wider audience, not just institutional traders with deep pockets. Automated trading systems powered by AI can scan multiple markets and execute trades, freeing traders from the need to monitor the markets constantly. This efficiency opens up day trading as a viable option for more people, potentially leading to additional income streams.

Continuous Learning and Adaptation

One of the most compelling aspects of AI is its capacity for continuous learning. Through machine learning algorithms, AI systems evolve by learning from market patterns, past trades, and changing conditions. This ability to adapt and refine strategies continuously keeps AI-enhanced trading relevant and effective, even as market dynamics shift.

In essence, the integration of AI into day trading is a game-changer. It amplifies human capabilities, mitigates human weaknesses, and opens up new avenues for strategy and success. As we stand on the brink of this new era, embracing AI in day trading is not just an advantage; it's becoming a necessity for those looking to stay competitive and achieve rapid gains in the fast-paced world of financial markets.

The Promise of Instant Wealth

The allure of day trading, particularly when enhanced by Artificial Intelligence (AI), often centers around the tantalizing promise of instant wealth. This notion conjures images of traders effortlessly amassing fortunes with the click of a button, capitalizing on the power of AI to navigate the complexities of the financial markets with unprecedented precision and speed. While this vision is compelling, it's essential to approach it with both optimism and a healthy dose of realism.

The Reality of Rapid Gains

AI-enhanced day trading can indeed lead to rapid gains, thanks to the advantages AI offers in terms of data analysis, speed of execution, and risk management. The ability of AI to process vast amounts of market data in real-time, predict trends, and execute trades at optimal moments can significantly increase the chances of making profitable trades within short periods.

Setting Realistic Expectations

However, the journey to instant wealth is not without its challenges and risks. The markets are inherently volatile and unpredictable, and while AI can mitigate some of this unpredictability, it cannot eliminate it entirely. Success in day trading, even with AI, requires a deep understanding of market dynamics, a well-thought-out strategy, and the discipline to stick to that strategy even in the face of market volatility.

The Importance of Strategy and Discipline

The most successful AI-enhanced traders are those who combine the power of AI with a robust trading strategy and strict risk management rules. They understand that while AI can provide a significant edge, it is not a magic bullet. Success requires a commitment to continuous learning, adapting strategies as market conditions change, and the patience to let the power of AI and compounding work over time.

Mitigating Risks

While the potential for rapid gains is real, so too is the risk of rapid losses. Effective risk management is crucial in day trading, perhaps even more so when leveraging AI. Setting stop-loss limits, diversifying trading strategies, and not overleveraging are essential practices to protect against significant losses.

The Long-Term Perspective

It's also important to adopt a long-term perspective. While day trading can indeed generate quick profits, viewing it as a path to instant wealth can lead to unrealistic expectations and rash decisions. Successful traders view their trading as a business, with AI as a powerful tool in their arsenal to grow their wealth steadily over time, rather than expecting overnight success.

Conclusion

The promise of instant wealth in AI-enhanced day trading is both exciting and possible, but it comes with caveats. The key to realizing this promise lies in leveraging AI's capabilities wisely, with a well-researched strategy, disciplined execution, and a commitment to ongoing learning and adaptation. By approaching day trading with realism, patience, and a focus on long-term growth, traders can harness the power of AI to not only achieve rapid gains but also build sustainable wealth.

Chapter 1: Day Trading Demystified

In the high-octane world of financial markets, day trading stands out as one of the most exhilarating and potentially rewarding activities. Yet, for many, it remains shrouded in mystery and misconceptions. This chapter aims to demystify day trading, laying a solid foundation for understanding its core principles, the role of AI in modern trading, and setting the stage for the transformative strategies that follow.

Section 1.1: Understanding Day Trading

Day trading involves buying and selling financial instruments within the same trading day. Traders capitalize on small price movements in highly liquid stocks or currencies, aiming to enter and exit positions for profit within the same day, avoiding the risk of overnight market fluctuations.

Key Characteristics:

- **Short-term Nature**: Positions are held for seconds, minutes, or hours but always closed by the end of the trading day.
- **Liquidity and Volatility**: Preferred stocks or assets are highly liquid and volatile, offering numerous trading opportunities.
- **High Frequency**: Many trades may be executed in a single day, leveraging small price gaps for profit.

Section 1.2: The Evolution of Day Trading

The advent of electronic trading platforms and the internet has democratized day trading, making it accessible to a broader audience beyond institutional traders and professionals. The evolution has been marked by significant milestones:

- **Pre-Internet Era**: Limited to professional traders due to high barriers to entry, including costly trading floors and information networks.
- **Online Trading Revolution**: The 1990s saw the rise of online brokerages, lowering costs and opening the market to retail traders.
- **AI and Algorithmic Trading**: Recent years have witnessed the integration of AI and algorithms, automating and optimizing trading strategies.

Section 1.3: Day Trading vs. Long-Term Investing

While both aim for profitability, day trading and long-term investing are fundamentally different approaches to the markets:

- **Time Horizon**: Day trading focuses on short-term gains within a single trading day, whereas long-term investing looks to compound returns over years or decades.
- **Risk Profile**: Day trading involves higher risk and requires active management. In contrast, long-term investing typically follows a "buy and hold" strategy, riding out market volatility.
- **Skill and Involvement**: Day trading demands a high level of skill, constant market monitoring, and quick

decision-making. Long-term investing relies more on fundamental analysis and is less time-intensive.

Section 1.4: The Role of the Day Trader

Day traders are not just participants in the financial markets; they contribute to market liquidity and efficiency. Their activities ensure that there are always buyers and sellers available, contributing to smoother price movements and more accurate market pricing.

Conclusion

Demystifying day trading reveals it as a dynamic, accessible, yet challenging arena. It requires not just an understanding of market principles but also a disciplined approach and the right tools, including the strategic use of AI, which we will explore in the coming chapters. As we delve deeper into the world of AI-enhanced day trading, remember that at its core, day trading is about leveraging opportunities within the market's inherent ebb and flow.

1.1 Understanding Day Trading

Day trading, often envisioned as the epitome of high-stakes financial maneuvering, is both an art and a science. It involves buying and selling financial instruments within the same trading day, capitalizing on small price movements to generate profits. This section aims to unpack the nuances of day trading, offering clarity on its workings, appeal, and the skills required to navigate this fast-paced trading environment.

The Essence of Day Trading

At its core, day trading is about exploiting short-term market fluctuations. Unlike long-term investors, day traders are not concerned with the intrinsic value of the assets they trade. Instead, they focus on predicting how stocks, currencies, or other financial instruments will move within hours or even minutes. This requires a keen sense of market trends, an understanding of trading volumes, and the ability to act swiftly on emerging opportunities.

Key Characteristics

- **Short-term Focus**: Positions are held for a very short duration, from a few seconds to a few hours, but always closed before the market closes to avoid overnight risks.
- **Liquidity and Volatility**: Day traders thrive on liquidity and volatility. Liquidity allows for the easy entry and exit of positions, while volatility provides the price movements necessary to make a profit.
- **Leverage**: Many day traders use leverage to amplify their trading capital, allowing for larger positions and potentially higher returns. However, this also increases the risk of significant losses.

Skills and Tools for Success

- **Analytical Skills**: A successful day trader analyzes market data, charts, and news to make informed decisions quickly.
- **Technical Analysis**: Many traders rely on technical analysis — using historical price data and chart patterns to predict future movements.

- **Discipline**: Day trading demands strict discipline to follow trading plans, manage risks, and know when to cut losses.
- **Emotional Control**: The ability to maintain composure and make objective decisions under pressure is crucial. Emotional decisions can lead to mistakes and financial loss.

The Role of Technology

Advancements in technology have significantly impacted day trading. High-speed internet and sophisticated trading platforms have democratized access, allowing individuals to trade from virtually anywhere. Furthermore, tools like real-time data feeds, advanced charting software, and automated trading systems have become indispensable in the modern trader's arsenal.

The Appeal of Day Trading

The allure of day trading lies in its potential for rapid financial gains. The prospect of turning a profit within a single day is attractive to many. However, it's important to note that day trading is not a guaranteed path to wealth. It carries high risks, and success requires dedication, continual learning, and a well-thought-out strategy.

Conclusion

Understanding day trading is the first step toward mastering its challenges and opportunities. It's a realm characterized by rapid movements, requiring a blend of analytical prowess, technological leverage, and psychological resilience. As we delve deeper into the intricacies of day trading, especially in the context of AI-enhanced strategies, this foundational knowledge will serve as a critical guidepost.

1.2 The Evolution of Day Trading

Day trading, as we know it today, is the culmination of decades of financial innovation, technological advancements, and regulatory changes. This evolution has transformed day trading from an activity once reserved for institutional players and well-capitalized individuals to an accessible and popular strategy for traders worldwide.

The Early Days

In the earliest stages, day trading was almost exclusively the domain of professional traders and financial institutions. Access to markets was limited, requiring significant capital, and the trading floor was the epicenter of activity. Information flowed through ticker tapes and telephones, and trades were executed through shouted orders and hand signals—a far cry from today's digital landscape.

The Electronic Revolution

The 1970s and 1980s marked the beginning of electronic trading, gradually replacing traditional open outcry systems. This period introduced electronic communication networks (ECNs), which allowed traders to bypass traditional market makers and execute trades directly with one another. This shift began to level the playing field, reducing costs and increasing market transparency.

The Internet Boom

The 1990s brought the internet boom, which was a pivotal moment for day trading. Online brokerages emerged, drastically lowering the cost of transactions and making real-time market data and trading tools accessible to the average person. This democratization of trading spurred a surge in day trading activity among retail investors.

The Rise of Algorithmic Trading

The early 21st century saw the rise of algorithmic trading, where trades are executed by complex algorithms and automated trading systems. This development was driven by advances in computing power and the availability of high-frequency trading platforms. Algorithmic trading introduced a new level of speed and efficiency, further intensifying the day trading environment.

The Impact of Regulation

Regulatory changes have also played a significant role in shaping day trading. In response to the volatility and risks associated with day trading, regulatory bodies worldwide have implemented measures to protect retail investors. These include the pattern day trader rule in the United States, which imposes minimum equity requirements on traders who execute a high number of trades.

The Advent of AI and Machine Learning

The latest chapter in the evolution of day trading involves the integration of artificial intelligence (AI) and machine learning. These technologies offer unprecedented analytical capabilities, enabling the analysis of vast datasets to identify trading opportunities and execute trades at speeds and precision unattainable by human traders. AI and machine learning are not only optimizing trading strategies but also revolutionizing risk management and predictive analytics.

Conclusion

The evolution of day trading is a testament to the relentless pace of technological and financial innovation. From the bustling trading floors of the past to today's AI-driven digital platforms, day trading has undergone a profound transformation. This journey has made day trading more accessible, efficient, and dynamic, offering new opportunities and challenges for traders in the digital age. As we look to the future, the continued advancement of technology, particularly in AI and machine learning, promises to further redefine the boundaries of day trading.

1.3 Day Trading vs. Long-Term Investing

Understanding the distinction between day trading and long-term investing is crucial for anyone venturing into the financial markets. While both strategies aim to generate profits, they differ fundamentally in their approach, time horizon, risk tolerance, and the skills required for success. This section explores these differences to provide a clearer perspective on which strategy might align best with your financial goals and temperament.

Time Horizon

- **Day Trading**: This strategy involves buying and selling financial instruments within the same trading day. Trades are rarely held overnight, and the primary goal is to capitalize on short-term market fluctuations. The focus is on the immediate market conditions and price movements.
- **Long-Term Investing**: In contrast, long-term investing involves holding assets for months, years, or even decades. The aim is to build wealth gradually through the compounding of earnings and dividends. Long-term investors are less concerned with short-term market volatility and more focused on the long-term growth potential of their investments.

Approach and Analysis

- **Day Trading**: Successful day trading relies heavily on technical analysis, which involves examining price charts, patterns, and various technical indicators to make trading decisions. Day traders need to stay abreast of market news and events that can cause immediate market moves.
- **Long-Term Investing**: Long-term investors often rely on fundamental analysis, which assesses the intrinsic value of an investment by examining related economic, financial, and other qualitative and quantitative factors. This approach involves a thorough analysis of the financial health, business model, industry position, and growth prospects of the entities in which they invest.

Risk and Return

- **Day Trading**: This strategy is generally considered higher risk due to the significant volatility in short-term market movements and the common use of leverage to amplify gains (and losses). The potential for high returns exists, but so does the risk of substantial losses, especially if a trader is inexperienced or lacks discipline.
- **Long-Term Investing**: Long-term investing tends to be less risky over time, as markets generally trend upwards in the long run, smoothing out short-term fluctuations. While the returns might be less dramatic in the short term compared to successful day trades, the compounding effect over years provides a potential for substantial growth with reduced volatility.

Required Skills and Temperament

- **Day Trading**: Requires the ability to make quick decisions, a deep understanding of market mechanics, and a high tolerance for risk. Emotional discipline is crucial to prevent rash decisions driven by fear or greed.
- **Long-Term Investing**: Demands patience, a thorough understanding of market fundamentals, and the resilience to hold steady through market ups and downs. Long-term investors need to resist the temptation to react to short-term market noise.

Capital Involvement

- **Day Trading**: Typically requires a significant amount of capital, especially to overcome the pattern day trader rule in the U.S., which mandates a minimum account balance of $25,000 for those who execute four or more day trades in five business days.
- **Long-Term Investing**: Can be started with less capital, and due to the compounding effect, even small, regular investments can grow significantly over time.

Conclusion

The choice between day trading and long-term investing should be based on individual financial goals, risk tolerance, available capital, time commitment, and personal interest in the markets. Day trading offers the thrill and potential for rapid gains but comes with higher risk and demands constant attention. Long-term investing, on the other hand, is more about steady growth and requires patience and a belief in the long-term potential of the markets. Each has its merits and challenges, and understanding these can help in making an informed decision that aligns with your financial aspirations.

Chapter 2: The AI Revolution in Trading

The advent of Artificial Intelligence (AI) in the financial markets has sparked a revolution, changing the face of trading as we know it. This chapter delves into the transformative impact of AI on trading, highlighting how it has enhanced analytical capabilities, decision-making processes, and overall market efficiency. From algorithmic trading to predictive analytics, AI is not just a tool but a game-changer in the fast-paced world of trading.

Section 2.1: Understanding AI and Its Components

AI encompasses a range of technologies that enable machines to mimic human intelligence, including learning, reasoning, and self-correction. Key components include:

- **Machine Learning (ML)**: An AI subset where algorithms learn from data, identify patterns, and make decisions with minimal human intervention.
- **Natural Language Processing (NLP)**: Enables computers to understand, interpret, and produce human language, crucial for analyzing news, reports, and social media.
- **Neural Networks**: Inspired by the human brain's structure, these networks can learn and improve over time, making them ideal for complex financial modeling.

Section 2.2: The Impact of AI on Trading Strategies

AI has redefined traditional trading strategies, introducing levels of speed, efficiency, and accuracy previously unattainable:

- **Algorithmic Trading**: AI-driven algorithms can execute trades at optimal times, based on criteria set by traders or learned from data, maximizing profits and minimizing losses.
- **High-Frequency Trading (HFT)**: AI enhances HFT, allowing for the analysis and execution of thousands of orders at unprecedented speeds, exploiting minute price differences.
- **Predictive Analytics**: AI's ability to sift through vast datasets enables the prediction of market trends and asset price movements, giving traders a significant advantage.

Section 2.3: AI's Role in Risk Management

Risk management is a critical aspect of trading where AI excels by:

- **Identifying Risk Factors**: AI algorithms can analyze a broader range of risk factors in real-time, from market trends to geopolitical events, offering a comprehensive risk assessment.
- **Portfolio Optimization**: AI can suggest portfolio adjustments, balancing between risk and reward to align with a trader's risk tolerance and investment goals.

- **Fraud Detection**: AI systems are adept at detecting unusual patterns that may indicate fraudulent activity, enhancing the security of trading operations.

Section 2.4: Ethical and Regulatory Considerations

As AI reshapes trading, it also raises ethical and regulatory questions:

- **Transparency**: The "black box" nature of some AI systems can make it difficult to understand how decisions are made, raising concerns about transparency and accountability.
- **Market Fairness**: The superior capabilities of AI can lead to concerns about market fairness, with well-resourced entities gaining a significant advantage over average traders.
- **Regulatory Challenges**: Regulators are tasked with ensuring that the use of AI in trading complies with existing laws and does not harm the market's integrity.

Section 2.5: The Future of AI in Trading

Looking ahead, the integration of AI in trading is set to deepen:

- **Advancements in AI Technologies**: Ongoing improvements in AI will further enhance trading strategies, risk management, and market analysis.
- **Democratization of AI Tools**: As AI tools become more accessible, a broader range of traders will be able to leverage these technologies, leveling the playing field.

- **Ethical AI Frameworks**: The development of ethical guidelines and frameworks for AI in trading will be crucial to address transparency, fairness, and accountability issues.

Conclusion

The AI revolution in trading has brought about unprecedented changes, enabling traders to navigate the markets with greater insight, efficiency, and profitability. While AI opens up new possibilities, it also presents challenges that need to be addressed, including ethical considerations and the need for regulatory frameworks. As we continue to explore the potential of AI in trading, it's clear that this technology will remain at the forefront of financial market evolution, reshaping strategies and operations in ways we are only beginning to understand.

2.1 What is AI and How Does It Work?

Artificial Intelligence (AI) is a transformative technology that is reshaping industries worldwide, with trading and finance being no exceptions. At its core, AI involves creating computer systems capable of performing tasks that typically require human intelligence. These tasks include learning from data, recognizing patterns, making decisions, and even understanding natural human language.

The Foundations of AI

AI is built on various interdisciplinary foundations, including computer science, mathematics, psychology, and neuroscience. These foundations have led to the development of algorithms and models that enable machines to process information and learn in ways that mimic human cognitive functions.

Key Components of AI in Trading

- **Machine Learning (ML)**: This subset of AI allows systems to learn from data, identify patterns, and make decisions with minimal human input. In trading, ML can be used to predict market trends, identify trading opportunities, and automate trading strategies.
- **Deep Learning**: A more complex subset of machine learning, deep learning uses neural networks with many layers (hence "deep") to analyze vast amounts of data. This is particularly useful in trading for processing complex market data and making predictive analyses.
- **Natural Language Processing (NLP)**: This AI capability enables computers to understand, interpret, and generate human language. In the context of trading, NLP can analyze financial news, reports, and social media to gauge market sentiment and predict potential market movements.

How AI Operates in Trading

1. **Data Ingestion**: AI systems start by ingesting vast amounts of data, which can include historical price data, financial news, economic indicators, and more.
2. **Data Processing and Analysis**: The AI then processes and analyzes this data using complex algorithms. Machine learning models, for instance, can be trained on historical data to identify patterns

or trends that may be indicative of future market movements.

3. **Learning and Adaptation**: AI systems are not static; they learn and adapt over time. As new data comes in, the AI updates its models and strategies based on outcomes and new information, continually refining its predictions and decisions.
4. **Decision Making**: In trading, the AI uses its analysis to make decisions, such as identifying the optimal time to buy or sell an asset. These decisions can be executed automatically by the system, enabling rapid responses to market changes.
5. **Continuous Improvement**: AI systems can be set up for continuous learning, meaning they refine their algorithms based on their success and failures, improving their accuracy and effectiveness over time.

The Role of AI in Enhancing Trading Strategies

AI's ability to process and analyze data at scale and speed surpasses human capabilities, providing traders with invaluable insights and the ability to execute trades at optimal times. Moreover, AI's predictive analytics can uncover opportunities and risks in the market that might not be visible to the human eye, allowing for more informed and strategic trading decisions.

Conclusion

AI represents a paradigm shift in how trading strategies are developed and executed. Its ability to learn from data, recognize patterns, and make informed decisions is transforming the trading landscape, making it more efficient, responsive, and profitable. As AI technology continues to evolve, its impact on trading is expected to grow, further embedding intelligence and automation into the fabric of financial markets.

2.2 The Impact of AI on Financial Markets

The integration of Artificial Intelligence (AI) into financial markets has been nothing short of revolutionary. AI's advanced computational and analytical capabilities have profoundly impacted how markets operate, influencing everything from individual trading strategies to the overall market structure. This section delves into the various ways AI has reshaped financial markets.

Enhanced Market Efficiency

AI contributes significantly to market efficiency, a core concept in financial economics that posits that asset prices fully reflect all available information. AI systems can process vast datasets—from market data to global news—in real time, ensuring that information is rapidly assimilated and reflected in market prices. This heightened efficiency aids in the accurate pricing of assets and helps reduce arbitrage opportunities, making markets more predictable and stable.

Algorithmic Trading and Liquidity

Algorithmic trading, powered by AI, has become a dominant force in financial markets. AI algorithms can execute complex trading strategies at speeds and volumes unattainable by human traders, significantly enhancing market liquidity. This liquidity is crucial for the smooth functioning of markets, as it ensures that trades can be executed quickly and at stable prices, even during volatile periods.

Predictive Analytics and Market Insights

AI excels in predictive analytics, leveraging historical and real-time data to forecast market trends and asset price movements. These insights are invaluable for traders and investors, enabling them to make more informed decisions. Beyond price predictions, AI's analytics can uncover deeper market insights, such as identifying emerging economic cycles or sectoral shifts, thereby adding a layer of strategic intelligence to market operations.

Risk Management

AI's impact extends to risk management, an essential aspect of financial operations. Through advanced modeling and simulation capabilities, AI systems can anticipate a range of risk factors and market scenarios, allowing institutions and individual traders to better prepare for potential market downturns. AI-enhanced risk management contributes to the resilience and stability of financial markets by enabling proactive rather than reactive measures.

Market Surveillance and Fraud Detection

Financial markets are susceptible to manipulative practices and fraudulent activities, which can undermine market integrity and investor confidence. AI-powered surveillance systems can monitor trading patterns in real time, identifying anomalies that may indicate market manipulation or fraud. This capability is critical for regulatory bodies and market operators in maintaining transparency and trust in financial markets.

Democratization of Trading

AI has played a role in democratizing access to financial markets. Sophisticated trading tools and analytics, once the preserve of institutional investors, are now more widely available thanks to AI-driven platforms. This accessibility enables a broader range of participants to engage in trading, contributing to market depth and diversity.

Challenges and Considerations

While AI's impact on financial markets is largely positive, it also presents challenges. The speed and complexity of AI-driven trading can amplify market volatility, and the "black box" nature of some AI models can obscure the rationale behind market movements, raising transparency concerns. Moreover, the reliance on historical data by AI models can sometimes lead to systemic biases or overlook unprecedented market conditions.

Conclusion

AI has indelibly transformed financial markets, enhancing efficiency, liquidity, and intelligence while also democratizing access to sophisticated trading tools. As AI technology evolves, its role in financial markets is set to expand, further influencing trading strategies, market operations, and regulatory frameworks. Navigating this AI-driven landscape requires a nuanced understanding of both its vast potential and its inherent challenges.

2.3 Real-World Success Stories

The transformative impact of Artificial Intelligence (AI) on financial markets is not just theoretical; it's evidenced by numerous real-world success stories. These instances highlight how AI's predictive analytics, algorithmic trading, and risk management capabilities have led to significant achievements in trading and investment strategies. Here, we explore a few emblematic success stories that underscore AI's potential in reshaping financial markets.

Quantitative Hedge Funds and AI

One of the most notable success stories in the realm of AI-driven finance comes from quantitative hedge funds, which rely heavily on algorithmic trading powered by AI and machine learning. Firms like Renaissance Technologies, Two Sigma, and DE Shaw have gained legendary status for their use of complex mathematical models and sophisticated algorithms to drive investment strategies, outperforming markets and delivering substantial returns to their investors. These firms have demonstrated the power of leveraging AI to analyze vast datasets, identifying patterns and correlations that are invisible to human analysts, thereby gaining a competitive edge in the markets.

AI in Asset Management

Beyond hedge funds, traditional asset management firms have also successfully integrated AI into their operations. BlackRock, the world's largest asset manager, launched AI-driven funds that use machine learning algorithms to select stocks, demonstrating AI's applicability in long-term investment strategies as well as short-term trading. These

AI-powered funds aim to optimize portfolio performance by dynamically adjusting to market changes, showcasing AI's potential to enhance decision-making in asset management.

AI for Personalized Trading and Investment

On the retail side, AI has enabled the creation of personalized trading and investment platforms that cater to individual preferences and risk profiles. Robo-advisors like Wealthfront and Betterment use AI algorithms to provide personalized investment advice and portfolio management services at a fraction of the cost of traditional financial advisors. These platforms have democratized access to sophisticated investment strategies, allowing a broader audience to benefit from AI's analytical prowess.

AI in Market Surveillance and Fraud Detection

The use of AI in market surveillance and fraud detection represents another success story, with regulatory bodies and exchanges employing AI systems to monitor trading patterns and flag suspicious activities. For instance, the Market Abuse Regulation (MAR) in Europe utilizes AI tools to enhance the detection of market manipulation and insider trading, contributing to fairer and more transparent markets.

Risk Management Breakthroughs

AI's role in risk management has also led to significant achievements. Financial institutions are increasingly using AI to model market risks and predict potential downturns, allowing for more proactive risk management strategies.

JPMorgan Chase's LOXM program is a prime example, where AI is used to execute trades optimally, minimizing market impact and transaction costs, thereby managing risk more effectively.

Conclusion

These real-world success stories are just the tip of the iceberg in demonstrating AI's vast potential and positive impact on financial markets. From hedge funds to personal finance, AI's ability to process and analyze data at an unprecedented scale and speed is unlocking new opportunities, optimizing strategies, and enhancing market integrity. As AI continues to evolve, it's expected to drive further innovations and successes in the complex world of finance.

Chapter 3: Preparing for AI-Enhanced Trading

Embracing AI-enhanced trading involves more than just an understanding of financial markets; it requires a strategic approach to integrating AI technologies into your trading practices. This chapter outlines essential steps and considerations for traders preparing to leverage AI in their trading strategies, ensuring a smooth transition and effective utilization of AI's capabilities.

Section 3.1: Building a Solid Foundation in Trading and AI

Before diving into AI-enhanced trading, it's crucial to have a solid grounding in both trading fundamentals and AI principles.

- **Understand Trading Basics**: Ensure a strong grasp of trading concepts, market dynamics, technical analysis, and risk management strategies. Knowledge of various financial instruments and market conditions is essential for informed decision-making.
- **Learn AI Basics**: Familiarize yourself with the basics of AI, including machine learning, neural networks, and natural language processing. Understanding how AI systems learn, process data, and make predictions is critical for leveraging AI in trading effectively.

Section 3.2: Choosing the Right AI Tools and Platforms

With a myriad of AI tools and platforms available, selecting the right ones for your trading needs is a critical step.

- **Research AI Trading Platforms**: Investigate various AI trading platforms to find one that aligns with your trading style and objectives. Consider platforms that offer robust data analytics, customizable trading algorithms, and user-friendly interfaces.
- **Evaluate AI Tools**: Look for AI tools that provide real-time market analysis, predictive analytics, and automated trading options. Tools that offer backtesting capabilities are particularly valuable for validating your trading strategies before executing them in live markets.

Section 3.3: Data Acquisition and Management

AI systems thrive on data. Having access to high-quality, relevant data is paramount for AI-enhanced trading.

- **Gather Comprehensive Market Data**: Collect extensive historical and real-time market data, including price movements, trading volumes, and economic indicators. The more data your AI system has to learn from, the more accurate its predictions and analyses will be.
- **Ensure Data Quality**: Verify the accuracy and reliability of your data sources. Inaccurate or incomplete data can lead to flawed analyses and misguided trading decisions.

Section 3.4: Developing and Testing AI Trading Strategies

With the right foundation, tools, and data, the next step is to develop and test AI-driven trading strategies.

- **Strategy Development**: Utilize AI tools to identify potential trading strategies based on historical data analysis and market trend predictions. Incorporate your trading preferences and risk tolerance into the strategy design.
- **Backtesting**: Test your AI-driven strategies using historical data to evaluate their effectiveness. Backtesting helps identify potential issues and optimize strategies before applying them to live trading.

Section 3.5: Continuous Learning and Adaptation

AI-enhanced trading is an ongoing learning process, both for the trader and the AI system.

- **Stay Informed**: Keep abreast of the latest developments in AI and financial markets. Continuous learning is key to adapting to new technologies and market changes.
- **Iterate and Optimize**: Regularly review and refine your AI trading strategies based on performance data and market feedback. AI systems can adapt over time, but human oversight is essential to guide these adaptations effectively.

Conclusion

Preparing for AI-enhanced trading is a multifaceted process that involves a deep understanding of both trading and AI, selecting appropriate tools, managing quality data, and continuously refining strategies. By approaching AI integration with a strategic and informed mindset, traders can harness the power of AI to enhance their trading decisions, manage risks more effectively, and potentially achieve greater returns in the fast-paced world of financial markets.

3.1 Essential Tools and Resources

As you embark on the journey of AI-enhanced trading, equipping yourself with the right tools and resources is paramount. This section outlines essential technologies, software, and educational materials that can significantly enhance your ability to effectively leverage AI in your trading strategies.

AI Trading Platforms

An AI trading platform is your primary tool, integrating various AI functionalities to analyze market data, predict trends, and execute trades. Look for platforms that offer:

- **Real-time Analytics**: Capability to analyze market data in real time, providing instant insights for swift decision-making.
- **Customizable Algorithms**: Flexibility to create or modify trading algorithms to fit your specific trading style and risk tolerance.

- **Backtesting Facilities**: Allowance for testing your trading strategies against historical data to assess their viability before live implementation.

Data Analytics Software

Data is the lifeblood of AI trading. High-quality analytics software can help you process and analyze vast datasets to uncover market insights. Key features to consider include:

- **Data Visualization Tools**: Graphical representation of data to help identify trends, patterns, and anomalies.
- **Statistical Analysis Capabilities**: Advanced statistical functions to dissect and understand market behaviors.
- **Integration Options**: Ability to integrate with various data sources and trading platforms for a seamless workflow.

Machine Learning Libraries and Frameworks

For those inclined towards a more hands-on approach with AI, familiarizing yourself with machine learning libraries and frameworks is beneficial. Popular options include:

- **TensorFlow**: An open-source library developed by Google, ideal for deep learning applications.
- **PyTorch**: Developed by Facebook, known for its flexibility and ease of use in research and development.
- **Scikit-learn**: A simple and efficient tool for data mining and data analysis, built on NumPy, SciPy, and matplotlib.

Financial Market Data Sources

Access to comprehensive and reliable market data is crucial for training your AI models. Consider subscribing to:

- **Historical Data Archives**: Databases that offer extensive historical market data for backtesting your strategies.
- **Real-time Data Feeds**: Services that provide real-time market data, ensuring your AI systems can react to market changes promptly.

Educational Resources

Staying informed about the latest trends in AI and trading is vital. Utilize:

- **Online Courses**: Platforms like Coursera, Udemy, and edX offer courses on AI, machine learning, and financial trading.
- **Specialized Forums and Communities**: Engage with communities on Reddit, Quora, and dedicated trading forums for insights and discussions.
- **Books and Academic Journals**: Stay updated with the latest research and insights by reading authoritative books and peer-reviewed journals in AI and finance.

Hardware Considerations

While cloud-based platforms often handle the heavy lifting, having a reliable computer with a fast processor and sufficient RAM can enhance your trading setup, especially for real-time data analysis and strategy development.

Conclusion

Building a robust toolkit is a critical step in preparing for AI-enhanced trading. By combining powerful AI trading platforms with comprehensive data analytics tools, advanced machine learning libraries, quality data sources, continuous learning resources, and suitable hardware, you equip yourself with the capabilities needed to navigate the complexities of AI-driven financial markets successfully.

3.2 Setting Up Your AI Trading Station

Creating an effective AI trading station is about more than just hardware and software; it's about crafting an environment that supports efficient, informed, and responsive trading activities. This section guides you through setting up a trading station that leverages AI to optimize your trading strategy and execution.

Hardware Requirements

An AI trading station demands robust hardware to handle real-time data processing, complex algorithmic calculations, and potentially, machine learning model training:

- **High-Performance Computer**: A fast processor (Intel i7/i9 or AMD Ryzen 7/9), at least 16GB RAM (32GB or more for heavy computations), and a solid-state drive (SSD) for quick access to data and applications.
- **Multiple Monitors**: Multiple high-resolution monitors allow you to monitor various data streams, trading platforms, and analytical tools

simultaneously, providing a comprehensive view of the market.

- **Reliable Internet Connection**: A high-speed, stable internet connection is crucial for real-time data streaming and executing trades without delays.

Software and Platforms

Choosing the right software and platforms is crucial for leveraging AI in your trading. Consider the following types:

- **AI Trading Platforms**: Platforms that offer integrated AI capabilities for market analysis, prediction, and automated trading. Look for platforms with a strong reputation, extensive tools, and user support.
- **Data Analytics Software**: Software that allows for in-depth data analysis and visualization. Options like Tableau, Microsoft Power BI, or even Python-based tools (for those comfortable with coding) are excellent choices.
- **Machine Learning Frameworks**: If you're inclined to develop or customize AI models, familiarize yourself with frameworks like TensorFlow, PyTorch, or Scikit-learn.

Data Feeds and APIs

Real-time and historical data are the lifeblood of AI trading:

- **Market Data Subscriptions**: Subscribe to reliable real-time data feeds for the markets you intend to trade. Ensure the data covers all necessary assets and indicators relevant to your strategy.

- **Brokerage APIs**: Ensure your brokerage offers an API for automated trading. The API should allow your AI system to execute trades based on the strategies you've developed or adopted.

Ergonomic and Efficient Workspace

The physical setup of your trading station can significantly impact your trading efficiency and comfort:

- **Ergonomic Furniture**: Invest in an ergonomic chair and desk to support long hours of trading with minimal physical strain.
- **Organized Layout**: Arrange your monitors, keyboard, mouse, and any other peripherals in a manner that minimizes clutter and maximizes efficiency. Each element should be within easy reach and view.

Security Measures

Securing your AI trading station is paramount to protect your data and financial assets:

- **Robust Security Software**: Use high-quality antivirus and firewall software to protect against malware and cyber attacks.
- **Data Encryption**: Ensure that your sensitive data, especially related to trades and financial information, is encrypted and securely stored.
- **Regular Backups**: Maintain regular backups of critical data and trading algorithms to prevent loss in case of hardware failure or other issues.

Continuous Learning and Adaptation Setup

AI and financial markets are constantly evolving. Set up a system for continuous learning:

- **Educational Resources**: Dedicate space or devices for accessing educational resources, webinars, online courses, and the latest research in AI trading.
- **Feedback Mechanisms**: Implement systems to track the performance of your trades and strategies, allowing for continuous feedback and refinement.

Conclusion

Setting up an AI trading station involves careful consideration of hardware, software, data, ergonomics, security, and continuous learning. By creating an environment that supports the high demands of AI-enhanced trading, you position yourself to take full advantage of AI's capabilities, ultimately aiming for more informed decisions, faster execution, and improved trading outcomes.

3.3 Understanding Market Data

In the realm of AI-enhanced trading, market data serves as the foundation upon which trading decisions are made and strategies are built. Grasping the various types of market data, their sources, and how to effectively utilize them is crucial for any trader looking to leverage AI in their trading activities. This section delves into the essentials of market data, providing insights into its significance and application in AI-driven trading environments.

Types of Market Data

Market data encompasses a wide array of information that traders use to analyze and predict market movements. Understanding these types is key to developing effective AI-enhanced trading strategies:

- **Price Data**: This includes historical and real-time prices of financial instruments, typically represented through open, high, low, close, and volume (OHLCV) data. Price data is fundamental for technical analysis and backtesting trading strategies.
- **Volume Data**: Volume, the number of units traded during a given period, is crucial for understanding market activity levels and liquidity, often used to confirm trends or signals identified in price movements.
- **Order Book Data**: This data shows pending buy and sell orders at different price levels for a financial instrument. It provides insights into market depth, liquidity, and potential support and resistance levels.
- **Fundamental Data**: For long-term strategies, fundamental data such as earnings reports, economic indicators, and company financials are vital. AI models can analyze this data to gauge the intrinsic value of assets.
- **News and Sentiment Data**: AI can process vast amounts of textual data from news articles, social media, and financial reports to gauge market sentiment. This data can be particularly valuable in predictive models that anticipate market reactions to news events.

Sources of Market Data

Access to accurate and timely market data is critical. Here are common sources:

- **Financial Exchanges**: Direct data feeds from stock, commodity, and currency exchanges offer the most accurate and timely information, albeit often at a higher cost.
- **Data Vendors**: Companies like Bloomberg, Thomson Reuters, and others aggregate data from multiple exchanges and provide additional services like analytics and news.
- **Brokerage APIs**: Many online brokers offer access to market data through their APIs, which can be a cost-effective solution for individual traders.
- **Public Data Sets**: Various organizations and platforms provide free access to historical market data, suitable for backtesting and initial strategy development.

Integrating Market Data with AI

To leverage market data effectively within AI-driven trading strategies, consider the following:

- **Data Cleaning and Preprocessing**: Raw market data often requires cleaning and formatting to be usable for AI models. This can include dealing with missing values, adjusting for corporate actions like splits, and normalizing data.
- **Feature Engineering**: Transforming market data into features that AI models can use to make predictions is an art and science. This can involve creating

technical indicators, sentiment scores, or custom metrics that encapsulate market behaviors.

- **Real-time Processing**: For strategies that rely on real-time data, ensure your AI system can process and analyze data quickly enough to capitalize on short-term market movements.

Conclusion

Market data is the lifeblood of AI-enhanced trading, providing the critical inputs needed for strategy development and execution. A deep understanding of the types of market data, their sources, and how to effectively integrate them into AI models is essential for traders looking to harness the power of AI in the financial markets. By meticulously selecting, processing, and analyzing market data, traders can improve the accuracy of their predictions and the effectiveness of their trading strategies.

Chapter 4: Crafting Winning AI Trading Strategies

The core of AI-enhanced trading lies in developing strategies that leverage artificial intelligence to outperform traditional methods. This chapter guides you through the process of crafting AI-driven trading strategies, from conceptualization to testing and implementation. The goal is to combine market knowledge, data insights, and AI capabilities to create dynamic strategies that adapt to market conditions and align with your trading objectives.

Section 4.1: Identifying Trading Opportunities with AI

The first step in crafting an AI trading strategy is to identify potential trading opportunities using AI's unique capabilities:

- **Market Pattern Recognition**: Use machine learning models to recognize complex market patterns and trends that may not be visible to the human eye.
- **Sentiment Analysis**: Implement natural language processing (NLP) to gauge market sentiment from news articles, social media, and financial reports, turning qualitative data into actionable insights.
- **Anomaly Detection**: Employ AI to identify anomalies in market data that could indicate unique trading opportunities or potential risks.

Section 4.2: Strategy Development

With potential opportunities identified, the next step is to develop a trading strategy that capitalizes on these insights:

- **Defining Trade Entry and Exit Points**: Use AI to determine optimal entry and exit points based on predictive models and market analysis, incorporating factors like price levels, volume, and sentiment.
- **Risk Management**: Integrate risk management rules into your AI models, setting parameters for stop-loss, take-profit, and position sizing based on the AI's risk assessment of each trade.
- **Portfolio Diversification**: Apply AI to portfolio management, ensuring a diversified investment strategy that balances risk across different assets and market conditions.

Section 4.3: Backtesting and Optimization

Before deploying an AI trading strategy live, it's crucial to backtest it against historical data:

- **Historical Simulation**: Run your AI strategy against historical market data to simulate its performance over various market conditions.
- **Performance Metrics**: Analyze key performance indicators (KPIs) such as return on investment (ROI), Sharpe ratio, drawdown, and win-loss ratios to assess the strategy's effectiveness.
- **Optimization**: Use the insights gained from backtesting to refine and optimize your strategy, adjusting AI model parameters, and trading rules as necessary.

Section 4.4: Live Testing and Implementation

Gradually transition from backtesting to live market conditions:

- **Paper Trading**: Start with paper trading, where your AI strategy trades in real-time markets without risking actual capital, allowing you to observe its performance in live conditions.
- **Small-Scale Implementation**: Once confident in the strategy's paper trading performance, begin trading with a small amount of capital to gauge its effectiveness in real conditions.
- **Continuous Monitoring and Adjustment**: Keep a close eye on the AI strategy's performance, ready to make adjustments as market conditions change or as new data becomes available.

Section 4.5: Ethical Considerations and Compliance

Ensure your AI trading strategy adheres to ethical guidelines and regulatory compliance:

- **Transparency**: Maintain transparency in how your AI models make trading decisions, especially if managing funds for others.
- **Fairness**: Avoid strategies that might manipulate market prices or disadvantage other market participants.
- **Regulatory Compliance**: Stay informed about and comply with trading regulations and guidelines, which can vary significantly between jurisdictions.

Conclusion

Crafting winning AI trading strategies requires a blend of market knowledge, data analytics, AI technology, and ethical considerations. By systematically identifying opportunities, developing strategies, backtesting, and cautiously implementing, traders can harness the power of AI to enhance their trading outcomes. Remember, the key to success lies in continuous learning, adaptation, and adherence to sound trading principles and ethical standards.

4.1 Basics of AI Trading Algorithms

AI trading algorithms are the cornerstone of AI-enhanced trading, offering a sophisticated approach to analyzing markets, predicting movements, and executing trades. Understanding the basics of these algorithms, including their types, development process, and key considerations, is essential for any trader looking to leverage AI in their strategy.

Types of AI Trading Algorithms

- **Predictive Models**: Utilize historical and real-time data to forecast future price movements. Techniques can range from simple linear regression to complex neural networks.
- **Classification Algorithms**: Identify patterns or conditions that lead to specific market events, such as significant price increases or decreases, by classifying data points based on historical precedents.
- **Reinforcement Learning**: An area of machine learning where algorithms learn optimal actions through trial and error, rewarding strategies that lead to favorable outcomes. Ideal for dynamic markets, as the algorithm adapts its strategy over time based on feedback from market performance.

- **Sentiment Analysis Models**: Leverage natural language processing (NLP) to analyze news headlines, social media, and financial reports, assessing market sentiment and its potential impact on asset prices.

Developing AI Trading Algorithms

1. **Objective Definition**: Clearly define what you aim to achieve with the algorithm, whether it's predicting price movements, identifying trading signals, or automating trade execution.
2. **Data Collection and Preparation**: Gather and prepare relevant data, which could include price data, volume, news articles, and economic indicators. Ensuring data quality is paramount for the algorithm's accuracy.
3. **Feature Selection and Engineering**: Identify the most relevant features that impact market movements. This may involve transforming raw data into more informative indicators or creating new features that better represent market dynamics.
4. **Model Selection**: Choose the appropriate AI model based on your trading objectives and the nature of your data. This could range from simpler models like decision trees to more complex ones like deep learning networks.
5. **Training and Validation**: Train your model on a portion of historical data and validate its performance on another set to ensure it generalizes well to unseen data.
6. **Backtesting**: Test the algorithm using historical data to simulate how it would have performed in the past.

This helps gauge its effectiveness and refine its parameters.

Key Considerations

- **Overfitting**: Beware of overfitting, where an algorithm performs well on historical data but fails to generalize to new data. Regularization techniques and proper validation can help mitigate this risk.
- **Execution Speed**: In markets where timing is crucial, the execution speed of your algorithm can significantly impact its effectiveness. Optimize code and consider hardware capabilities to minimize latency.
- **Risk Management**: Incorporate risk management directly into your AI algorithms, setting parameters for maximum drawdown, stop-loss levels, and position sizing to protect your capital.
- **Ethical and Regulatory Compliance**: Ensure that your trading algorithm complies with market regulations and ethical guidelines, avoiding strategies that could manipulate market prices or disadvantage other participants.

Conclusion

The development of AI trading algorithms involves a systematic process from defining objectives to rigorous backtesting. By understanding the types of algorithms available and adhering to best practices in development and risk management, traders can create effective AI-driven strategies that enhance decision-making and potentially improve trading outcomes. Continuous monitoring, updating, and refining are crucial as market conditions evolve and new data becomes available.

4.2 Developing Your First AI Strategy

Embarking on the journey to develop your first AI trading strategy is an exciting endeavor that combines finance, data science, and machine learning. This process involves several key steps, from understanding the market and selecting the right data to training your model and backtesting your strategy. Here's a structured approach to help you develop your first AI trading strategy effectively.

Understanding Market Dynamics

Before diving into AI, it's crucial to have a clear understanding of the market you intend to trade in. Different markets (stocks, forex, commodities) have unique characteristics and factors that drive price movements. Familiarize yourself with these dynamics, as they will inform the type of data you collect and the features you create for your AI model.

Data Collection and Preparation

- **Select Relevant Data**: Depending on your market analysis, choose data that will likely influence market movements. This might include price data, trading volume, economic indicators, news articles, and social media sentiment.
- **Data Cleaning**: Ensure your data is clean and reliable. This involves handling missing values, removing outliers, and ensuring data consistency.

- **Feature Engineering**: Transform your raw data into features that your AI model can use. This might involve calculating technical indicators like moving averages or RSI, or deriving sentiment scores from textual data.

Choosing the Right AI Model

- **Start Simple**: Begin with simpler models like linear regression or decision trees to establish a baseline performance. These models are easier to interpret and can provide valuable insights.
- **Experiment with Complexity**: As you become more comfortable, experiment with more complex models such as ensemble methods (Random Forests) or neural networks. These models can capture more complex patterns but require more data and computational power.

Model Training and Validation

- **Split Your Data**: Divide your data into training, validation, and test sets. A common split is 70% training, 15% validation, and 15% test.
- **Training**: Use the training set to teach your model to recognize patterns that predict market movements.
- **Validation**: Use the validation set to tune your model's hyperparameters and avoid overfitting. This process helps ensure that your model generalizes well to new data.

Backtesting Your Strategy

- **Historical Simulation**: Apply your trained model to the test set, which should simulate unseen market conditions, to evaluate how your strategy would have performed historically.
- **Performance Metrics**: Assess your strategy using metrics such as return on investment (ROI), Sharpe ratio, maximum drawdown, and win/loss ratios. This evaluation will help you understand the risk and return profile of your strategy.

Refinement and Iteration

- **Iterate and Improve**: Based on backtesting results, refine your model and strategy. This might involve adding new features, trying different models, or adjusting your risk management rules.
- **Continuous Learning**: Stay informed about new developments in AI and financial markets. Continuously update your model with new data and insights to maintain its relevance and effectiveness.

Considerations for Live Trading

- **Start Small**: When you transition to live trading, start with a small amount of capital to test your strategy under real market conditions.
- **Monitor Performance**: Closely monitor your strategy's performance and be prepared to make adjustments as needed. Market conditions can change, and your model may need to be updated.

Conclusion

Developing your first AI trading strategy is a process of exploration, learning, and continuous improvement. By understanding market dynamics, carefully preparing your data, and methodically training and testing your model, you can create an AI strategy that enhances your trading decisions. Remember, success in AI trading requires not just technical skills but also a deep understanding of financial markets and a disciplined approach to risk management.

4.3 Backtesting for Success

Backtesting is a critical step in the development of any AI trading strategy, serving as a bridge between theoretical models and real-world performance. It involves simulating a trading strategy using historical data to determine how it would have performed in the past. This process helps validate the effectiveness of the strategy and identifies areas for improvement before risking actual capital in live trading.

Setting Up Your Backtesting Environment

1. **Historical Data**: Ensure you have access to high-quality historical market data that matches the markets and time frame your AI strategy is designed to trade. This data should include all relevant features your model uses, such as price, volume, and any external indicators.
2. **Simulation Engine**: Use or develop a backtesting engine that can accurately simulate market conditions and the execution of trades. The engine

should account for factors like transaction costs, slippage, and market impact.

3. **Strategy Implementation**: Implement your AI trading strategy within the backtesting environment, ensuring that the simulation accurately reflects the strategy's trading rules and decision-making process.

Conducting the Backtest

- **Run Simulations**: Execute your AI strategy against the historical data, recording trade entries, exits, and outcomes. It's crucial to simulate the strategy over a range of market conditions to understand its behavior in different environments.
- **Adjust for Realism**: Incorporate realistic trading constraints into your backtest, such as transaction costs, order fill assumptions, and liquidity considerations. These factors can significantly impact the perceived performance of your strategy.

Analyzing Backtest Results

- **Performance Metrics**: Evaluate the strategy's performance using a variety of metrics, including total return, Sharpe ratio, maximum drawdown, and win-loss ratio. These metrics provide insights into the strategy's risk-reward profile and its consistency over time.
- **Benchmarking**: Compare your strategy's performance against relevant benchmarks, such as market indices or the performance of similar strategies. This comparison can help contextualize the effectiveness of your AI model.

- **Overfitting Detection**: Be vigilant for signs of overfitting, where the model performs exceptionally well on historical data but may not generalize to unseen data. Techniques like cross-validation and out-of-sample testing can help mitigate this risk.

Refining Your Strategy

- **Iterative Improvement**: Use insights gained from backtesting to refine your strategy. This might involve tweaking model parameters, enhancing feature selection, or adjusting risk management rules.
- **Robustness Checks**: Conduct additional tests to ensure the strategy's robustness, such as stress testing against extreme market scenarios or sensitivity analysis on key parameters.
- **Forward Testing**: Consider forward testing (paper trading) your refined strategy in real-time markets without using actual capital. This approach provides further validation under current market conditions.

Conclusion

Backtesting is an indispensable tool in the AI trading strategy development process, offering a risk-free way to gauge a strategy's potential effectiveness. By carefully setting up and conducting backtests, analyzing results critically, and using these insights for iterative refinement, traders can enhance the likelihood of success for their AI-driven strategies. Remember, a strategy's past performance is not always indicative of future results, so continuous monitoring and adaptation are key when transitioning to live trading.

Chapter 5: Risk Management in AI Day Trading

In the volatile realm of day trading, where market conditions can shift rapidly, integrating robust risk management practices is paramount, especially when leveraging AI technologies. Effective risk management ensures the longevity and sustainability of your trading strategy, protecting your capital from significant losses. This chapter outlines essential risk management principles and practices tailored for AI-enhanced day trading.

Understanding Risk in AI Trading

1. **Market Risk**: The risk of losses due to market fluctuations. AI models, while predictive, cannot guarantee future market movements, making exposure to sudden market changes inevitable.
2. **Model Risk**: The risk that an AI model's assumptions and predictions may not hold true in real market conditions, leading to unexpected losses.
3. **Operational Risk**: Includes risks related to technical failures, such as software bugs, connectivity issues, or data inaccuracies, which can impair trading operations.

Setting Risk Limits

- **Stop-Loss Orders**: Establish automatic stop-loss orders to limit the loss on any single trade. AI algorithms can dynamically adjust stop-loss levels based on changing market conditions and volatility.

- **Maximum Drawdown**: Define a maximum drawdown level for your trading account to limit overall losses over a specific period. This helps prevent significant depletion of your trading capital.

Diversification

- **Across Assets**: Spread your trades across different financial instruments to avoid concentrated exposure to a single asset's performance.
- **Strategic Diversification**: Employ multiple AI trading strategies that are uncorrelated or have different market assumptions. This approach can balance out performance across varying market conditions.

Regular Monitoring and Adjustments

- **Real-Time Monitoring**: Continuously monitor your AI trading system's performance and market conditions. Be prepared to intervene manually if market conditions deviate significantly from your model's assumptions.
- **Periodic Review**: Regularly review and update your AI models and risk parameters to align with evolving market dynamics and your trading performance.

Stress Testing and Scenario Analysis

- **Stress Testing**: Simulate your AI trading strategies against extreme market conditions (e.g., financial crises, flash crashes) to understand potential vulnerabilities and adjust your risk parameters accordingly.

- **Scenario Analysis**: Evaluate your strategy's performance under various hypothetical market scenarios to anticipate potential risks and outcomes.

Incorporating Risk Management into AI Models

- **Dynamic Risk Adjustment**: Integrate risk management directly into your AI models, allowing them to adjust trading activities based on real-time risk assessments and market volatility.
- **Leverage Management**: Use AI to optimize leverage ratios, ensuring they align with your risk tolerance and market conditions, mitigating the risk of significant losses due to highly leveraged positions.

Legal and Regulatory Compliance

- **Stay Informed**: Keep abreast of legal and regulatory requirements related to day trading and AI in your jurisdiction. Compliance with these regulations is crucial to avoid legal repercussions and ensure the integrity of your trading operations.
- **Ethical Trading Practices**: Ensure your AI trading strategies adhere to ethical standards, avoiding manipulative practices that could distort market prices or disadvantage other market participants.

Conclusion

Risk management is an integral component of a successful AI day trading strategy. By understanding the unique risks associated with AI trading, setting clear risk limits, diversifying strategically, and incorporating risk management directly into your AI models, you can safeguard your capital against significant losses. Regular monitoring, stress testing, and adherence to legal and regulatory standards further reinforce the stability and reliability of your trading operations, enabling a disciplined and sustainable approach to AI-enhanced day trading.

5.1 Identifying and Managing Risks

In the fast-paced world of AI day trading, identifying and effectively managing risks is critical to safeguarding your investments and ensuring long-term success. This section delves into common risks associated with AI trading and provides strategies for mitigating these risks, thereby fostering a more secure and resilient trading environment.

Market Risk

- **Volatility**: Sudden price swings can lead to significant losses, especially in leveraged positions.
  - o *Mitigation*: Utilize volatility indicators within AI models to adjust trading strategies dynamically, reducing exposure during high volatility periods.
- **Liquidity Risk**: The risk of being unable to execute trades at desired prices due to insufficient market liquidity.
  - o *Mitigation*: Develop AI models to assess liquidity in real-time and limit orders to assets with adequate liquidity.

Model Risk

- **Overfitting**: AI models that perform well on historical data but fail to generalize to new data can lead to unexpected losses.
  - *Mitigation*: Use techniques like cross-validation and regularize models to prevent overfitting. Continuously update models with new data and validate their performance out-of-sample.
- **Model Obsolescence**: Financial markets evolve, and models that do not adapt can become obsolete.
  - *Mitigation*: Implement adaptive learning within AI models to update their parameters based on new market conditions and data.

Operational Risk

- **Technical Failures**: Software bugs, hardware failures, or connectivity issues can disrupt trading operations.
  - *Mitigation*: Establish robust IT infrastructure with redundancy and failover systems. Regularly update and test software to ensure reliability.
- **Data Integrity**: Inaccurate or incomplete data can lead to flawed trading decisions.
  - *Mitigation*: Implement rigorous data validation and cleaning processes. Use multiple data sources to verify the accuracy of critical information.

Systemic Risk

- **Regulatory Changes**: New regulations or changes in existing laws can impact trading strategies and operations.
  - *Mitigation*: Stay informed about regulatory developments and adjust trading strategies to ensure compliance.
- **Market Events**: Unforeseen events like geopolitical developments or economic crises can lead to widespread market disruptions.
  - *Mitigation*: Incorporate global news and event monitoring into AI models to react swiftly to unforeseen events. Maintain diversified portfolios to mitigate the impact of systemic market events.

Leverage Risk

- **Excessive Leverage**: Using high leverage can amplify gains but also losses, potentially leading to rapid account depletion.
  - *Mitigation*: Implement AI-driven leverage optimization, calibrating leverage levels based on market volatility and individual trade risk.

Psychological Risk

- **Emotional Trading**: Emotional decision-making can lead to irrational trades, deviating from a disciplined strategy.
  - *Mitigation*: Rely on AI-driven decision-making to maintain objectivity. Set predefined risk parameters and adhere to them strictly.

Legal and Compliance Risk

- **Non-compliance**: Failing to adhere to trading regulations can result in penalties and trading restrictions.
  - *Mitigation*: Ensure AI trading systems are programmed to operate within regulatory guidelines. Regularly review compliance measures.

Conclusion

Identifying and managing the various risks associated with AI day trading is essential for protecting your capital and achieving consistent trading performance. By implementing targeted risk mitigation strategies, from enhancing model robustness to ensuring operational reliability and regulatory compliance, traders can navigate the complexities of the financial markets more safely and effectively. Continuous monitoring and adaptation are key, as the dynamic nature of markets and trading technologies demands an agile and informed approach to risk management.

5.2 The Role of AI in Risk Assessment

Artificial Intelligence (AI) plays a transformative role in risk assessment within the realm of day trading, offering advanced capabilities to identify, analyze, and mitigate various forms of risk. By leveraging AI, traders can gain deeper insights into market dynamics, enhance decision-making processes, and implement more effective risk management strategies. This section explores the multifaceted role of AI in assessing and managing trading risks.

Predictive Risk Modeling

AI's predictive analytics capabilities allow for the development of sophisticated models that forecast potential market movements and volatility, providing traders with an anticipatory tool to manage market risk.

- **Volatility Prediction**: AI models can analyze historical and real-time market data to predict future volatility, enabling traders to adjust their strategies accordingly.
- **Price Movement Forecasting**: By identifying patterns in market data, AI can predict short-term price movements, offering traders valuable insights to inform their trading decisions and manage exposure.

Real-time Risk Monitoring

AI systems can monitor a wide array of market and trade data in real-time, providing immediate insights into emerging risks and enabling rapid response to mitigate potential losses.

- **Market Anomalies Detection**: AI algorithms can detect unusual market behavior that may indicate heightened risk, allowing for prompt adjustments to trading positions.
- **Portfolio Risk Analysis**: AI tools continuously assess portfolio exposure to various risks, ensuring

diversification and balance in line with a trader's risk tolerance.

Quantitative Risk Management

AI enhances quantitative risk management techniques by providing more accurate and nuanced assessments of risk factors associated with trading strategies and financial instruments.

- **Value at Risk (VaR) Calculation**: AI models improve the accuracy of VaR calculations, offering a probabilistic assessment of potential losses under normal market conditions.
- **Stress Testing**: AI can simulate a range of extreme market scenarios to test the resilience of trading strategies, helping traders understand potential vulnerabilities.

Behavioral Risk Analysis

Beyond quantitative measures, AI can assess behavioral risks by analyzing trader behaviors and market sentiment, offering insights into psychological factors that may impact trading performance.

- **Trader Behavior Monitoring**: AI systems can identify patterns in a trader's decision-making that may indicate behavioral biases or emotional trading, prompting corrective actions.
- **Sentiment Analysis**: By analyzing news, social media, and financial reports, AI can gauge market sentiment, providing an additional layer of risk

assessment related to public perception and market reactions.

Compliance and Regulatory Risk

AI contributes to managing compliance and regulatory risk by ensuring trading activities adhere to established rules and regulations, thereby avoiding legal penalties and maintaining market integrity.

- **Regulatory Compliance Monitoring**: AI systems can monitor trading activities in real-time to ensure compliance with trading rules and regulations, flagging potential violations for review.
- **Fraud Detection**: AI algorithms can detect patterns indicative of fraudulent activities, protecting against manipulation and other illicit practices that could pose legal and financial risks.

Conclusion

The role of AI in risk assessment is multifaceted and profoundly impactful, offering advanced tools and techniques to navigate the complexities of day trading risk management. By leveraging AI for predictive modeling, real-time monitoring, quantitative and behavioral analysis, and compliance oversight, traders can achieve a more comprehensive and effective approach to managing risks. As AI technologies continue to evolve, their integration into risk assessment processes will undoubtedly become even more integral to successful trading strategies, enhancing both performance and security in the fast-paced trading environment.

5.3 Building a Risk Management Plan

A well-structured risk management plan is essential for navigating the uncertainties of the financial markets, especially in the high-stakes environment of AI day trading. This plan serves as a roadmap for identifying, assessing, and mitigating risks, ensuring that your trading strategy remains robust and sustainable over time. Here's a comprehensive guide to building an effective risk management plan tailored for AI-enhanced trading.

Define Your Risk Tolerance

- **Assess your financial goals and constraints** to establish a clear understanding of how much risk you're willing and able to take.
- **Risk per trade**: Determine the maximum percentage of your capital that you're willing to risk on a single trade.
- **Total exposure**: Set limits on the total amount of capital at risk at any given time across all open positions.

Identify Potential Risks

- **Market Risk**: Consider factors like volatility, liquidity, and market sentiment that could impact your trading positions.
- **Model Risk**: Assess the potential for model inaccuracies, overfitting, and assumptions that may not hold in real-market conditions.
- **Operational Risk**: Identify technical issues, data inaccuracies, and execution failures that could disrupt trading activities.

- **Systemic and Regulatory Risks**: Be aware of broader market changes, regulatory updates, and geopolitical events that could affect the trading environment.

Develop Risk Mitigation Strategies

- **Diversification**: Spread your investments across various assets, sectors, or strategies to reduce exposure to any single source of risk.
- **Stop-Loss Orders**: Implement automated stop-loss orders to limit potential losses on individual trades.
- **Position Sizing**: Use AI models to dynamically adjust position sizes based on current market volatility and individual trade risk.
- **Hedging**: Consider hedging strategies to offset potential losses in your trading positions with complementary positions.

Integrate AI for Dynamic Risk Management

- **Real-time Monitoring**: Utilize AI algorithms to monitor market conditions, portfolio performance, and risk exposure in real-time, allowing for immediate adjustments.
- **Predictive Analytics**: Leverage AI to forecast market trends and volatility, informing proactive risk management decisions.
- **Stress Testing**: Regularly test your AI models and trading strategies against extreme market scenarios to evaluate resilience and adjust risk parameters accordingly.

Establish a Review and Adjustment Process

- **Continuous Monitoring**: Keep a constant watch on your risk exposure and the performance of your risk management strategies, ready to make real-time adjustments as needed.
- **Regular Review**: Set periodic review intervals to assess the overall effectiveness of your risk management plan, incorporating lessons learned and adapting to changing market conditions.
- **Feedback Loop**: Create a feedback mechanism to learn from both successful and unsuccessful trades, refining your risk management strategies based on empirical evidence.

Documentation and Compliance

- **Document your plan**: Clearly outline your risk management strategies, decision-making processes, and compliance protocols.
- **Regulatory Adherence**: Ensure that your trading activities and risk management practices comply with relevant regulatory requirements and industry best practices.

Conclusion

Building a comprehensive risk management plan is a critical component of a successful AI day trading strategy. By clearly defining your risk tolerance, identifying potential risks, developing mitigation strategies, and leveraging AI for dynamic risk management, you can protect your capital and navigate market uncertainties more effectively. Regular review and adaptation of your plan, informed by continuous monitoring and empirical learning, will further enhance its effectiveness, ensuring long-term sustainability and resilience in your trading endeavors.

Chapter 6: Accelerating Your Gains with AI

In the dynamic world of trading, AI offers unprecedented opportunities to enhance decision-making, optimize strategies, and ultimately, accelerate gains. This chapter delves into how AI can be harnessed to not only manage risks but also to identify and exploit trading opportunities more effectively, leading to improved performance and profitability.

Leverage AI for Market Analysis

- **Advanced Pattern Recognition**: AI algorithms excel at identifying complex patterns and trends in market data that might be invisible to the human eye. Use these insights to make informed trading decisions.
- **Sentiment Analysis**: Utilize NLP (Natural Language Processing) to analyze news, social media, and financial reports, gauging market sentiment and its potential impact on asset prices.

Optimize Trade Execution

- **High-Frequency Trading (HFT)**: AI can execute orders at optimal times, capitalizing on minute price discrepancies and market inefficiencies for quick gains.
- **Smart Order Routing**: AI algorithms can analyze multiple trading venues in real time, routing orders to where they can be executed most favorably, considering factors like price, liquidity, and costs.

Enhance Portfolio Management

- **Dynamic Portfolio Adjustment**: Use AI to continually assess and adjust your portfolio composition based on real-time market conditions and risk assessments, ensuring alignment with your investment goals and risk tolerance.
- **Diversification Analysis**: AI can analyze historical and current market data to recommend diversification strategies that minimize risk while optimizing returns.

Utilize Predictive Analytics

- **Price Prediction Models**: Develop AI models that predict future price movements based on historical data and market indicators, giving you a competitive edge in timing your trades.
- **Event-Driven Trading**: Implement AI systems that can anticipate market reactions to scheduled events (like earnings reports or economic indicators releases) and unscheduled events (such as geopolitical developments).

Automate and Scale Trading Strategies

- **Algorithmic Trading**: Automate your trading strategies using AI, allowing for the execution of complex strategies at scale that would be impossible to manage manually.
- **Scalability**: AI enables the scaling of successful strategies across multiple markets and assets, increasing potential gains without a proportional increase in effort.

Continuous Learning and Adaptation

- **Adaptive Learning**: Implement machine learning algorithms that adapt and optimize their parameters in real-time based on market performance and feedback.
- **Backtesting and Forward Testing**: Regularly backtest your AI models against historical data and forward-test in live markets to ensure continued effectiveness and adaptability.

Ethical Considerations and Compliance

- **Ensure Ethical Use**: Maintain transparency in how AI models make trading decisions and avoid strategies that could manipulate market prices or disadvantage other market participants.
- **Regulatory Compliance**: Stay updated with and adhere to trading regulations and guidelines, especially concerning the use of AI in trading.

Conclusion

Harnessing AI in trading offers a path to accelerating gains through sophisticated market analysis, optimized trade execution, enhanced portfolio management, and predictive analytics. By automating and scaling effective strategies, and ensuring continuous learning and adaptation, traders can significantly enhance their trading performance. However, it's essential to balance the pursuit of gains with ethical considerations and regulatory compliance, ensuring sustainable and responsible trading practices.

6.1 Leveraging AI for Rapid Analysis

In the realm of day trading, where market conditions can change in milliseconds, the ability to analyze data rapidly and accurately provides a significant competitive advantage. Artificial Intelligence (AI) stands out as a powerful tool in this context, enabling traders to process and interpret vast amounts of market data at speeds unattainable by human capabilities. This section explores how AI can be leveraged for rapid analysis, enhancing decision-making and identifying opportunities more swiftly.

Real-time Data Processing

AI systems are adept at handling real-time data streams, from price movements and trading volumes to news updates and social media sentiment. By employing advanced algorithms, AI can sift through this deluge of information, highlighting relevant trends and anomalies that warrant attention, all in real time.

- **Streamlined Data Integration**: AI can aggregate data from multiple sources, providing a comprehensive market overview that informs more holistic trading decisions.
- **Anomaly Detection**: AI algorithms can quickly identify unusual market patterns or behaviors, potentially signaling lucrative trading opportunities or emerging risks.

Advanced Pattern Recognition

One of AI's most powerful capabilities is its ability to recognize complex patterns within large datasets. In trading, this translates to identifying profitable trends and signals amidst the market's noise.

- **Predictive Modeling**: Utilize machine learning models to predict future market movements based on historical data patterns.
- **Technical Analysis Automation**: Automate the identification of technical indicators and chart patterns, allowing for the rapid assessment of potential trade setups.

Sentiment Analysis

AI's Natural Language Processing (NLP) capabilities enable the analysis of textual data, providing insights into market sentiment that can influence trading decisions.

- **News and Reports Analysis**: Automatically analyze financial news and reports to gauge their potential impact on market movements.
- **Social Media Sentiment**: Monitor and analyze social media platforms for real-time public sentiment, offering immediate insights into market perceptions and reactions.

High-Speed Decision Making

AI not only analyzes data rapidly but also aids in swift decision-making, a critical component in the fast-paced trading environment.

- **Automated Trade Recommendations**: Generate real-time trade recommendations based on the AI's analysis, allowing traders to act quickly on emerging opportunities.

- **Risk Assessment**: Instantly evaluate the risk associated with potential trades, factoring in current market conditions and historical performance.

Scalability and Flexibility

The scalable nature of AI systems means that rapid analysis can be extended across multiple markets and assets simultaneously, without compromising speed or accuracy.

- **Multi-Asset Analysis**: Apply AI to analyze various asset classes concurrently, identifying opportunities across a broader market spectrum.
- **Adaptive Algorithms**: Ensure your AI systems can adapt to changing market conditions, maintaining their effectiveness in rapid analysis over time.

Conclusion

Leveraging AI for rapid analysis in day trading offers a profound advantage, enabling traders to process vast amounts of information quickly, identify patterns and trends, and make informed decisions with greater speed and confidence. By harnessing AI's capabilities in real-time data processing, advanced pattern recognition, sentiment analysis, and high-speed decision-making, traders can navigate the markets more effectively, capitalizing on opportunities as they arise. As AI technology continues to evolve, its role in facilitating rapid analysis and enhancing trading strategies is set to become even more integral.

6.2 Advanced AI Trading Techniques

As traders increasingly incorporate AI into their strategies, exploring advanced techniques becomes essential for maintaining a competitive edge. These sophisticated approaches leverage the full potential of AI, offering nuanced insights and enhanced decision-making capabilities. This section delves into several advanced AI trading techniques that can significantly elevate your trading performance.

Machine Learning Algorithms for Market Prediction

- **Deep Learning**: Utilize deep neural networks to model complex market behaviors and predict future price movements. Deep learning excels in capturing nonlinear relationships within vast datasets.
- **Reinforcement Learning**: Implement reinforcement learning models that learn optimal trading strategies through trial and error, dynamically adjusting based on market feedback and rewards.

Natural Language Processing (NLP) for Sentiment Analysis

- **Advanced Sentiment Analysis**: Go beyond basic positive or negative sentiment by analyzing the intensity and context of sentiments expressed in news articles, social media, and financial reports. This nuanced analysis can provide deeper insights into market sentiment.
- **Event Extraction**: Use NLP to identify and interpret key financial events from textual data, such as earnings announcements or regulatory changes,

assessing their potential impact on market movements.

Quantitative and Statistical Models

- **Bayesian Networks**: Apply Bayesian networks to model the probabilistic relationships among various market factors, offering a powerful framework for decision-making under uncertainty.
- **Time Series Analysis**: Employ advanced time series analysis techniques, like ARIMA (AutoRegressive Integrated Moving Average) or GARCH (Generalized Autoregressive Conditional Heteroskedasticity), to model and forecast market volatility.

Algorithmic Trading and High-Frequency Trading (HFT)

- **Adaptive Algorithms**: Develop algorithms that can adapt to changing market conditions in real time, optimizing trading strategies on the fly for maximum effectiveness.
- **Latency Reduction**: In HFT, minimizing latency is crucial. Optimize your trading infrastructure and employ AI to make split-second trading decisions, capitalizing on fleeting market opportunities.

Portfolio Optimization and Asset Allocation

- **AI-Driven Portfolio Management**: Use AI to dynamically adjust portfolio compositions, balancing risk and return in real-time based on market conditions and individual investment goals.
- **Risk Parity and Asset Allocation**: Implement AI models to achieve risk parity in your portfolio,

ensuring that assets are weighted according to their risk contribution, enhancing diversification and risk-adjusted returns.

AI for Risk Management

- **Predictive Risk Modeling**: Leverage AI to build predictive models that assess potential risks and their impact on your trading strategies, allowing for proactive risk management.
- **Dynamic Risk Adjustment**: Use AI to continuously evaluate and adjust risk levels in your trading strategy based on live market data, ensuring alignment with your risk tolerance.

Integration with Blockchain and Cryptocurrencies

- **Cryptocurrency Trading**: Apply AI techniques to the cryptocurrency market, analyzing blockchain data, transaction volumes, and social media sentiment to inform trading decisions.
- **Smart Contracts for Automated Execution**: Utilize blockchain technology and smart contracts to automate trade execution and settlement, enhancing efficiency and security.

Conclusion

Advanced AI trading techniques offer a multitude of benefits, from enhanced predictive accuracy and nuanced sentiment analysis to optimized portfolio management and cutting-edge risk assessment. By harnessing these sophisticated AI capabilities, traders can navigate the complexities of the financial markets with greater precision, agility, and confidence. As AI technology continues to evolve, staying abreast of and integrating these advanced techniques will be crucial for maintaining a competitive edge in the dynamic world of trading.

6.3 Scaling Your Trading Operations

Scaling your trading operations with AI involves expanding your trading strategies to manage larger volumes, more assets, or more complex strategies without proportionately increasing your risk or operational overhead. Effective scaling can lead to increased profitability and a more robust trading operation. Here's how AI can facilitate this growth.

Automating Trading Strategies

- **Full Automation**: Utilize AI to fully automate your trading strategies, from analysis to order execution, allowing you to handle larger transaction volumes efficiently.
- **Strategy Replication**: Apply successful trading models across different markets or asset classes, leveraging AI's adaptability to optimize strategies for each unique market condition.

Enhancing Analytical Capabilities

- **Big Data Analysis**: Employ AI to process and analyze vast amounts of market data from diverse sources, gaining insights that can drive multiple trading strategies simultaneously.
- **Predictive Modeling**: Use AI to develop and refine predictive models for various assets, enhancing the

accuracy of your forecasts and the scalability of your operations.

Risk Management at Scale

- **Dynamic Risk Adjustment**: Implement AI systems that continuously assess and adjust for risk in real-time across your entire portfolio, ensuring that your risk exposure remains within acceptable limits as you scale.
- **Portfolio Optimization**: Use AI to dynamically optimize your portfolio, balancing diversification and risk to maintain optimal performance as your operations grow.

Expanding Market Reach

- **Global Market Analysis**: Leverage AI to analyze global markets, identifying opportunities for geographic expansion of your trading activities.
- **Cross-Asset Strategies**: Utilize AI to develop and manage cross-asset trading strategies, diversifying your operations and spreading risk across different types of investments.

Improving Execution Speed and Efficiency

- **High-Frequency Trading (HFT)**: For strategies that rely on speed, use AI to minimize latency and maximize execution speed, capitalizing on short-term market inefficiencies.
- **Smart Order Routing**: Implement AI-driven order routing to ensure trades are executed at the best possible prices, enhancing profitability as you scale.

Leveraging Cloud Computing and Infrastructure

- **Cloud-Based Solutions**: Use cloud computing to scale your trading infrastructure flexibly and cost-effectively, accommodating increased data processing and storage needs without significant upfront investment.
- **Distributed Computing**: Employ distributed computing techniques to parallelize data processing and trading tasks, improving the scalability and reliability of your trading operations.

Continuous Learning and Adaptation

- **Adaptive Algorithms**: Ensure your AI models can adapt to changing market conditions, continuously learning from new data to maintain their effectiveness as you scale.
- **Backtesting and Forward Testing**: Regularly test your scaled strategies using historical and real-time data to ensure they perform as expected under various market conditions.

Compliance and Security

- **Regulatory Compliance**: As you scale, ensure your trading operations comply with all relevant regulations in the markets you operate, maintaining the integrity and legality of your trading activities.
- **Enhanced Security Measures**: Implement advanced security protocols and infrastructure to protect your growing operations from cyber threats and data breaches.

Conclusion

Scaling your trading operations with AI involves more than just increasing transaction volumes; it requires strategic enhancements to your analytical capabilities, risk management, market reach, and execution efficiency. By leveraging AI, cloud computing, and adaptive algorithms, you can expand your trading activities effectively, maintaining or even improving your profitability and risk profile. Continuous learning, testing, and compliance are crucial to ensuring sustainable growth in your trading operations.

Chapter 7: The Pitfalls of AI Day Trading

While AI day trading offers numerous advantages, it's not without its challenges and potential pitfalls. Recognizing and understanding these risks is crucial for traders looking to leverage AI effectively. This chapter discusses common pitfalls in AI day trading and provides insights on how to navigate or mitigate these issues.

Overreliance on AI

- **Human Oversight**: Completely relying on AI for decision-making can be risky. It's important to maintain human oversight to interpret AI suggestions and make final decisions, especially in unpredictable market conditions.
- **Understanding Limitations**: AI models are based on historical data and may not always predict future events accurately. Traders should understand the models' limitations and be prepared for unexpected market movements.

Model Overfitting

- **Complexity vs. Performance**: Creating overly complex models might lead to overfitting, where the model performs well on historical data but poorly on new, unseen data.
- **Regularization and Cross-Validation**: Implement regularization techniques and cross-validation to prevent overfitting, ensuring that models remain generalizable to new data.

Data Quality and Availability

- **Inaccurate Data**: AI models are only as good as the data they're trained on. Inaccurate or incomplete data can lead to misleading conclusions and poor trading performance.
- **Data Accessibility**: Access to real-time, high-quality data can be expensive, and limitations in data availability can hinder the effectiveness of AI models.

Market Dynamics and Black Swan Events

- **Unpredictable Markets**: AI models may not account for rare, unpredictable events (Black Swan events) that can dramatically impact markets.
- **Adaptability**: Ensure that your AI models can adapt quickly or that you have mechanisms in place to intervene manually during extreme market conditions.

Technological and Operational Risks

- **Infrastructure Failures**: Hardware malfunctions, software bugs, or connectivity issues can disrupt trading operations, leading to potential losses.
- **Cybersecurity Threats**: As AI systems rely heavily on technology, they are susceptible to cyber-attacks, which can compromise trading strategies and sensitive data.

Ethical and Regulatory Considerations

- **Algorithmic Bias**: AI models can inadvertently develop biases based on historical data, leading to unethical trading practices.
- **Regulatory Compliance**: Navigating the evolving landscape of regulations governing AI and trading is essential to avoid legal penalties and ensure fair trading practices.

Emotional and Psychological Factors

- **Overconfidence**: Success with AI trading models can lead to overconfidence, potentially encouraging riskier trades that do not align with one's risk management strategy.
- **Detachment from Trading**: Relying heavily on automation can lead to a detachment from the markets, potentially resulting in a loss of intuition and market sense developed through active trading.

Conclusion

AI day trading, while offering significant opportunities for efficiency and profitability, is fraught with potential pitfalls that can undermine success. By maintaining a balanced approach that includes human oversight, understanding AI limitations, ensuring data quality, preparing for market unpredictability, and adhering to ethical and regulatory standards, traders can mitigate these risks. Continuous learning, regular model evaluation, and adaptability are key to navigating the complexities of AI day trading and achieving long-term success.

7.1 Common Mistakes to Avoid

Embarking on AI day trading can be a challenging yet rewarding endeavor. However, certain common mistakes can hinder success and lead to unnecessary losses. Being aware of these pitfalls can help traders navigate the complexities of using AI in trading more effectively. This section highlights some of the most common mistakes to avoid in AI day trading.

Overcomplicating Your AI Model

- **Simplicity is Key**: Beginners often believe that more complex models guarantee better results. In reality, simpler models are easier to understand, debug, and often more effective.
- **Focus on Essentials**: Start with basic models and gradually add complexity only if it significantly improves performance.

Neglecting Data Quality and Preparation

- **Garbage In, Garbage Out**: The quality of your AI model's output is directly related to the quality of the input data. Ensure your data is clean, accurate, and relevant.
- **Comprehensive Data Preparation**: Spend ample time on data cleaning, normalization, and feature engineering to enhance model performance.

Ignoring Model Overfitting

- **Balance Fit and Generalization**: An overfitted model performs well on historical data but poorly on new data. Use techniques like cross-validation and keep test datasets strictly isolated to prevent overfitting.

- **Regular Model Updates**: Continuously monitor and update your model to adapt to changing market conditions.

Underestimating the Importance of Risk Management

- **Incorporate Risk Controls**: Every AI trading strategy should include robust risk management controls, such as stop-loss orders and position sizing, to protect against significant losses.
- **Dynamic Risk Assessment**: Use AI to dynamically assess and adjust risk levels in real-time based on evolving market conditions.

Overreliance on Backtesting

- **Historical Performance Isn't Future Proof**: Solely relying on backtesting results can be misleading. Markets evolve, and strategies that worked in the past may not work in the future.
- **Forward Testing**: Complement backtesting with paper trading or small-scale live trading to validate your strategy in current market conditions.

Ignoring Market and Model Anomalies

- **Stay Alert**: AI models can sometimes produce unexpected results due to anomalies in the data or market conditions. Regularly review trades to identify and investigate any anomalies.

- **Anomaly Detection Systems**: Implement systems to automatically detect and alert you to unusual model predictions or market conditions.

Failing to Stay Updated with Market and Regulatory Changes

- **Continuous Learning**: The financial markets and regulatory environment are constantly evolving. Stay informed about changes that could impact your trading strategy.
- **Compliance is Crucial**: Ensure your trading practices adhere to current regulations to avoid legal complications.

Neglecting Infrastructure Reliability and Security

- **Robust Infrastructure**: Ensure your trading setup, including hardware and internet connection, is reliable to avoid downtime during critical trading periods.
- **Cybersecurity Measures**: Implement strong security protocols to protect your trading system and sensitive data from cyber threats.

Conclusion

Avoiding common mistakes in AI day trading involves a combination of technical diligence, risk awareness, and operational reliability. By focusing on model simplicity, data quality, risk management, and continuous learning, traders can enhance the effectiveness of their AI trading strategies. Regular monitoring and adaptation, along with a commitment to security and compliance, further support sustainable trading success in the dynamic and fast-paced world of day trading.

7.2 Navigating Market Volatility

Market volatility is an inherent aspect of trading that can both present opportunities and pose significant risks. In the context of AI day trading, volatility requires careful navigation to harness its potential while safeguarding against the pitfalls it may present. This section explores strategies and considerations for effectively dealing with market volatility when using AI in your trading approach.

Understanding Volatility

- **Volatility as an Indicator**: Recognize that volatility is not inherently negative; it can indicate market opportunities as well as risks. High volatility often means greater price movements, which can lead to significant gains if managed correctly.
- **Volatility Sources**: Stay informed about factors that can cause sudden market volatility, including economic announcements, geopolitical events, and market sentiment shifts.

AI-Driven Volatility Analysis

- **Volatility Modeling**: Use AI models to analyze historical and real-time data to understand typical volatility patterns for different assets. Incorporating machine learning can help predict volatility spikes based on identified patterns.
- **Sentiment Analysis for Volatility Cues**: Leverage NLP to analyze news and social media in real-time,

identifying potential triggers for market volatility before they fully impact the market.

Adapting Strategies to Volatility

- **Dynamic Trading Rules**: Adjust your AI trading strategies dynamically based on current volatility levels. For instance, widen stop-loss thresholds during high volatility periods to avoid premature exits due to normal price fluctuations.
- **Volatility-Adjusted Position Sizing**: Use AI models to adjust position sizes based on the current volatility, reducing exposure during highly volatile periods to manage risk effectively.

Risk Management in Volatile Markets

- **Enhanced Risk Controls**: Implement more stringent risk management measures during periods of high volatility. This could include lowering leverage, increasing cash reserves, or using options for hedging.
- **Real-Time Monitoring**: Ensure your AI system includes real-time monitoring capabilities to quickly detect and respond to sudden market changes, safeguarding your positions.

Diversification to Mitigate Volatility Impact

- **Cross-Asset Diversification**: Spread your investments across different asset classes, which can react differently to the same market events, reducing overall portfolio volatility.

- **Strategic Diversification**: Employ multiple AI trading strategies that thrive under different market conditions. While some strategies may underperform during high volatility, others might capitalize on it.

Building Volatility-Resilient AI Models

- **Stress Testing**: Regularly test your AI models against historical periods of high volatility to assess their performance and resilience under such conditions.
- **Continuous Learning**: Incorporate mechanisms for your AI models to learn from new volatility patterns, enhancing their predictive accuracy and strategic responsiveness over time.

Emotional and Psychological Considerations

- **Maintain Discipline**: Volatile markets can test traders' emotions. Rely on your AI-driven strategies and pre-defined risk management rules to make objective decisions, avoiding impulsive reactions to market swings.
- **Psychological Preparedness**: Being mentally prepared for the heightened stress of trading in volatile markets is crucial. Ensure you have strategies in place to maintain focus and objectivity.

Conclusion

Effectively navigating market volatility with AI requires a comprehensive approach that includes advanced analytical techniques, adaptable trading strategies, stringent risk management, and a focus on emotional discipline. By understanding the nature of volatility and leveraging AI to analyze, predict, and respond to volatile market conditions, traders can position themselves to capitalize on opportunities while minimizing risks, even in the most turbulent markets.

7.3 Ethical Considerations

As AI continues to transform the landscape of day trading, ethical considerations come to the forefront, ensuring that these advanced technologies are used responsibly and fairly. This section addresses the ethical dimensions of AI in day trading, highlighting the importance of transparency, fairness, and accountability in deploying AI-driven trading strategies.

Transparency in AI Decision-Making

- **Explainability**: While AI models, especially deep learning networks, can be highly effective, they're often seen as "black boxes" due to their complexity. Striving for model explainability helps stakeholders understand how decisions are made, fostering trust.
- **Disclosure**: Be open about the use of AI in trading strategies, particularly if managing funds for others. Clients and regulatory bodies should be aware of the extent to which AI influences trading decisions.

Fairness and Market Integrity

- **Avoiding Market Manipulation**: Ensure that your AI strategies do not inadvertently manipulate market prices or exploit market inefficiencies in ways that could be deemed unfair or unethical.

- **Equal Access**: Consider the implications of AI technologies creating disparities in market access. High-frequency trading (HFT) and sophisticated AI algorithms can widen the gap between retail and institutional traders.

Data Privacy and Security

- **Responsible Data Use**: When using AI models that rely on large datasets, including personal or sensitive information, it's crucial to adhere to data privacy laws and ethical guidelines, ensuring that individuals' data is protected.
- **Security Measures**: Implement robust cybersecurity measures to protect your trading systems and data from unauthorized access, reducing the risk of data breaches that could compromise client information and capital.

Accountability and Responsibility

- **Human Oversight**: Maintain human oversight of AI trading systems to ensure that decisions align with ethical standards and regulatory requirements. The final accountability for AI-driven decisions should rest with human operators.
- **Regulatory Compliance**: Stay abreast of and comply with existing regulations governing AI and trading. Engage with regulatory bodies to contribute to the development of guidelines that ensure ethical AI use in financial markets.

Avoiding Bias

- **Bias Detection and Mitigation**: AI models can inadvertently learn and amplify biases present in historical data, leading to skewed decisions. Regularly audit models for bias and implement corrective measures to promote fairness.
- **Diverse Data and Perspectives**: Use diverse datasets and involve a range of perspectives in model development to reduce the risk of bias and ensure more balanced decision-making.

Continuous Ethical Evaluation

- **Ethical Review Processes**: Establish ongoing review processes to evaluate the ethical implications of AI trading strategies, adapting approaches as necessary to align with evolving ethical standards.
- **Engagement with Ethical Standards**: Participate in industry-wide discussions on ethical AI use, contributing to and adhering to established ethical frameworks and best practices.

Conclusion

Ethical considerations in AI day trading encompass a broad range of issues, from ensuring transparency and fairness to protecting data privacy and maintaining market integrity. As AI technologies become increasingly integral to trading strategies, it's imperative for traders and institutions to navigate these ethical dimensions responsibly, ensuring that the pursuit of profitability does not overshadow the importance of ethical conduct and societal impact. By prioritizing ethical considerations and engaging in ongoing ethical evaluation, the trading community can harness the power of AI in a manner that is not only effective but also principled and sustainable.

Chapter 8: Staying Ahead: The Future of AI in Day Trading

The integration of Artificial Intelligence (AI) in day trading is not a static landscape but an evolving frontier, continually shaped by advancements in technology, shifts in market dynamics, and changes in regulatory frameworks. Staying ahead in this rapidly changing environment requires an adaptive approach, a commitment to continuous learning, and an openness to innovation. This chapter explores what the future might hold for AI in day trading and how traders can prepare for and influence these upcoming changes.

Emerging Technologies and Innovations

- **Quantum Computing**: The advent of quantum computing could revolutionize data processing and analysis, offering the potential for even more sophisticated and rapid AI trading algorithms.
- **Blockchain and Decentralized Finance (DeFi)**: Blockchain technology and the rise of DeFi are creating new trading platforms and financial instruments, expanding the scope of AI trading strategies.
- **Augmented and Virtual Reality (AR/VR)**: AR/VR technologies could transform the way traders visualize and interact with market data, offering immersive and intuitive platforms for trading analysis.

Advances in AI and Machine Learning

- **Explainable AI (XAI)**: Advances in XAI aim to make AI decision-making processes more transparent and understandable, addressing the "black box" issue and potentially increasing trust in AI trading systems.
- **Autonomous Learning Systems**: Future AI systems may be capable of autonomous learning, continuously adapting their trading strategies without the need for explicit reprogramming, enhancing responsiveness to market changes.

Regulatory and Ethical Developments

- **Global AI Governance**: As AI becomes more prevalent in trading, expect more comprehensive global regulations focusing on ethical AI use, transparency, accountability, and data privacy.
- **Ethical AI Frameworks**: The development of ethical AI frameworks specific to trading could guide the responsible use of AI, ensuring fairness, integrity, and the protection of market participants.

Personalization and Democratization

- **Customizable AI Trading Assistants**: AI technologies could become more personalized, offering individual traders AI assistants tailored to their trading styles, preferences, and risk tolerance.
- **Wider Accessibility**: Continued advancements in AI could democratize sophisticated trading strategies, making powerful tools accessible to a broader range of traders, reducing the gap between retail and institutional participants.

Preparing for the Future

- **Continuous Education**: Stay informed about the latest developments in AI, finance, and technology through courses, webinars, and professional networks.
- **Collaborative Innovation**: Engage in collaborative projects and communities that focus on the intersection of AI and trading, contributing to and benefiting from collective knowledge and innovation.
- **Adaptive Mindset**: Cultivate an adaptive mindset, ready to explore new technologies, adapt to regulatory changes, and embrace innovative trading strategies.

Shaping the Future

- **Contribute to Ethical Standards**: Participate in discussions and initiatives that shape ethical standards and best practices for AI in trading, ensuring the technology is used responsibly and beneficially.
- **Feedback and Collaboration with Regulators**: Engage with regulatory bodies, providing feedback and insights from the trading community to help shape policies that foster innovation while protecting market integrity and participants.

Conclusion

The future of AI in day trading promises significant advancements and opportunities, driven by technological innovations, regulatory developments, and a shift towards more personalized and democratized trading tools. Staying ahead in this evolving landscape requires a proactive approach, embracing continuous learning, innovation, and ethical considerations. By preparing for and contributing to the future of AI in day trading, traders can not only navigate upcoming changes effectively but also play a role in shaping a responsible, innovative, and inclusive trading environment.

8.1 Emerging Trends in AI and Trading

The intersection of AI and trading is a dynamic field, continuously evolving with technological advancements and changing market landscapes. Staying informed about emerging trends is crucial for traders looking to leverage AI effectively. This section explores some of the most promising trends in AI and trading, offering insights into future possibilities and areas of growth.

AI-Driven Personalization in Trading Platforms

- **Customized Trading Experiences**: Future trading platforms may offer highly personalized experiences, using AI to tailor interfaces, tools, and information feeds to individual trader preferences and behaviors, enhancing usability and decision-making.
- **Behavioral Analytics**: AI could analyze traders' behavior patterns to offer customized strategy recommendations, risk management tips, and educational content, fostering more informed and confident trading decisions.

Integration of Alternative Data in Trading Strategies

- **Expanding Data Sources**: Traders are increasingly incorporating alternative data sources—such as satellite imagery, IoT device data, and social media sentiment—into their trading strategies for a more comprehensive market view.
- **AI for Data Synthesis**: AI technologies, especially those specializing in big data analytics, will play a crucial role in synthesizing and extracting actionable insights from diverse and unconventional data sets.

Advances in Predictive Analytics and Machine Learning

- **Enhanced Predictive Models**: Continuous advancements in machine learning algorithms are expected to improve the accuracy and reliability of predictive models in forecasting market movements and identifying trading opportunities.
- **Self-Improving Algorithms**: The development of algorithms that can self-optimize and learn from their performance in real-time will enable more adaptive and resilient trading strategies.

Decentralized Finance (DeFi) and Blockchain

- **Blockchain in Trading**: Blockchain technology offers increased transparency, security, and efficiency in trading operations. AI could enhance blockchain-based trading platforms by providing advanced analysis and automated trading capabilities.
- **AI in DeFi**: The DeFi space, characterized by its innovation and rapid growth, presents a fertile ground for AI applications, from optimizing liquidity

pools to predicting market trends in token ecosystems.

Quantum Computing's Impact on Trading

- **Quantum Advantage**: Quantum computing holds the potential to process complex financial models and vast datasets at unprecedented speeds, offering new horizons in market analysis and strategy optimization.
- **Security Implications**: The advent of quantum computing also raises concerns about data security and encryption, necessitating new cryptographic standards to protect financial data.

Ethical AI and Regulatory Compliance

- **Focus on Ethical AI**: As AI becomes more prevalent in trading, there will be a heightened focus on developing and implementing AI systems that adhere to ethical guidelines, ensuring fairness, transparency, and accountability.
- **Adapting to AI Regulations**: Regulatory frameworks governing the use of AI in trading will continue to evolve, requiring traders to stay informed and compliant with new policies and standards.

Cross-Disciplinary AI Applications

- **Interdisciplinary Innovation**: The fusion of AI with fields like behavioral finance, psychology, and environmental science could lead to novel trading strategies that consider a wider range of factors, from trader psychology to global sustainability trends.

Conclusion

Emerging trends in AI and trading point towards a future where personalized trading experiences, advanced predictive analytics, integration of alternative data, and the application of groundbreaking technologies like blockchain and quantum computing redefine the trading landscape. As these trends continue to evolve, they offer traders new tools and strategies for market analysis, risk management, and execution. Staying abreast of these developments and understanding their implications will be key for traders aiming to leverage AI for competitive advantage and sustainable success in the markets.

8.2 Continuous Learning and Adaptation

In the rapidly evolving landscape of AI-enhanced trading, continuous learning and adaptation are not just beneficial—they're essential for sustained success. As market dynamics shift and AI technologies advance, traders must remain agile, constantly updating their knowledge and adjusting their strategies to maintain a competitive edge. This section explores strategies for fostering an environment of continuous learning and adaptation in the context of AI day trading.

Embracing a Culture of Learning

- **Stay Curious**: Cultivate a mindset that is open to new ideas, technologies, and methodologies.

Embrace the rapid changes in AI and trading as opportunities for growth.

- **Lifelong Education**: Commit to ongoing education through courses, webinars, workshops, and conferences focused on AI, trading, and related fields. Online platforms like Coursera, Udemy, and edX offer a wealth of resources.

Leveraging Community and Collaborative Learning

- **Join Trading and AI Communities**: Engage with online forums, social media groups, and professional networks where traders and AI enthusiasts share insights, strategies, and experiences.
- **Collaboration**: Seek opportunities to collaborate on projects or participate in trading competitions. Collaborative environments can offer diverse perspectives and accelerated learning.

Staying Informed About Market and Technological Trends

- **Regular Market Analysis**: Keep abreast of market trends, economic indicators, and geopolitical events that could impact trading strategies. Utilize AI tools to assist in this analysis, ensuring a comprehensive understanding of market conditions.
- **Technology Watch**: Stay updated on advancements in AI, machine learning, data analytics, and related technologies. Consider subscribing to relevant newsletters, journals, and industry publications.

Implementing Adaptive AI Models

- **Dynamic Strategy Optimization**: Use AI models capable of adapting to changing market conditions. These models should continuously learn from new data, optimizing strategies to maintain their effectiveness over time.
- **Feedback Mechanisms**: Incorporate feedback loops into your AI systems, allowing them to learn from their successes and failures. This iterative process is crucial for refining models and strategies.

Experimentation and Testing

- **Innovate and Experiment**: Don't shy away from experimenting with new AI technologies, data sources, or trading strategies. Innovation is key to discovering competitive advantages in the market.
- **Rigorous Backtesting and Forward Testing**: Continually test new strategies against historical data and in simulated environments. This practice not only validates their effectiveness but also provides insights for further refinement.

Reflective Practice and Review

- **Regular Performance Reviews**: Conduct periodic reviews of your trading performance, AI model accuracy, and strategy effectiveness. Use these reviews to identify areas for improvement and adjustment.
- **Reflective Learning**: After each significant trading decision or outcome, take the time to reflect on what

was learned, what could be improved, and how insights gained can be applied to future strategies.

Adaptability to Regulatory Changes

- **Regulatory Compliance**: Monitor and adapt to regulatory changes affecting AI and trading. Ensure that your trading practices remain compliant, ethical, and aligned with industry standards.

Conclusion

Continuous learning and adaptation are fundamental to thriving in the AI-enhanced trading landscape. By fostering a culture of learning, engaging in collaborative environments, staying informed about market and technological advancements, and implementing adaptive AI models, traders can navigate the complexities of the market more effectively. Regular experimentation, reflective practice, and adherence to regulatory standards further support a trader's ability to evolve and succeed in the dynamic world of AI day trading.

8.3 Joining the Community of AI Traders

Engaging with the community of AI traders offers invaluable opportunities for knowledge exchange, collaboration, and networking. This vibrant community comprises individuals and organizations at the forefront of combining AI with trading strategies, exploring innovative solutions, and pushing the boundaries of what's possible in financial markets. This section guides you on how to become an active participant in this community and leverage the collective wisdom and experiences it offers.

Identify Relevant Communities and Platforms

- **Online Forums and Social Media**: Platforms like Reddit, Discord, and LinkedIn host numerous groups dedicated to AI trading, where members share insights, strategies, and the latest industry news.
- **Specialized Websites and Blogs**: Follow websites and blogs focused on AI trading. These can be excellent sources of detailed analyses, case studies, and expert opinions.

Attend Conferences and Webinars

- **Industry Conferences**: Attend conferences related to AI, machine learning, finance, and trading. Events like the AI in Finance Summit or QuantCon are great places to meet like-minded professionals and learn from industry leaders.
- **Online Webinars and Workshops**: Participate in webinars and workshops that delve into specific aspects of AI trading. These sessions often provide practical knowledge and allow for real-time interaction with experts.

Engage in Collaborative Projects and Competitions

- **Open Source Projects**: Contribute to or start open-source projects related to AI trading. Platforms like GitHub offer a space for collaborative development and innovation.
- **Trading Competitions**: Participate in trading competitions, which often involve developing and testing AI trading strategies under real-world conditions. These competitions can provide a

practical testing ground and a chance to learn from peers.

Continuous Learning and Skill Development

- **Educational Courses**: Enroll in courses that cover AI, machine learning, data science, and financial trading. Continuous skill development is key to staying relevant in the fast-evolving field of AI trading.
- **Research Publications**: Stay updated with the latest research by reading academic papers and attending seminars. Institutions and journals often publish cutting-edge work in AI and financial trading.

Networking and Mentorship

- **Build Relationships**: Networking with other traders and AI enthusiasts can open doors to mentorship opportunities, collaborative ventures, and even potential partnerships.
- **Mentorship**: Seek mentors who have proven experience in AI trading. Their guidance can be invaluable in navigating challenges and accelerating your learning curve.

Share Knowledge and Contribute

- **Active Participation**: Don't just be a passive observer. Engage actively by asking questions, sharing your experiences, and contributing to discussions. Your unique insights could be valuable to others.
- **Content Creation**: Consider creating and sharing content, such as blog posts, tutorials, or case studies,

about your experiences and experiments in AI trading. Sharing your journey can help others and establish your presence in the community.

Conclusion

Joining and actively participating in the community of AI traders can significantly enhance your learning journey, offering access to a wealth of collective knowledge, cutting-edge ideas, and networking opportunities. By engaging in collaborative projects, continuous learning, and knowledge sharing, you can contribute to and benefit from the community's collective progress. The relationships and insights gained through this community can be instrumental in navigating the complexities of AI-enhanced trading and achieving long-term success.

Conclusion

As we journey through the dynamic and intricate world of AI-enhanced day trading, it's evident that the fusion of artificial intelligence with financial trading is not just a fleeting trend but a paradigm shift that's reshaping the landscape of the financial markets. From leveraging AI for rapid market analysis and developing advanced trading algorithms to navigating the challenges of market volatility and ethical considerations, the integration of AI technologies offers unprecedented opportunities for traders to enhance their strategies, manage risks more effectively, and achieve greater profitability.

The key to thriving in this evolving environment lies in continuous learning and adaptation, staying informed about emerging trends, and actively engaging with the community of AI traders. By embracing the potential of AI, while also being mindful of its limitations and ethical implications, traders can navigate the complexities of the market with greater insight and agility.

As we close this exploration of AI in day trading, I hope you've found the insights and strategies discussed here valuable and empowering. Whether you're a seasoned trader looking to integrate AI into your strategies or a newcomer intrigued by the possibilities AI trading offers, there's no doubt that we're on the cusp of a new era in financial trading.

If you've found this guide helpful, I would greatly appreciate it if you could take a moment to leave a review on Amazon. Your feedback not only supports my work but also helps others discover and navigate the exciting possibilities of AI-enhanced day trading. Together, let's continue to learn, innovate, and push the boundaries of what's possible in the world of trading.

Thank you for joining me on this journey, and here's to your success in the dynamic world of AI day trading!

A Preview of "Escape the 9-to-5: Build Your Fortune with Proven Options Trading Strategies"

"Escape the 9-to-5" is not merely a title; it embodies a promise of freedom, financial independence, and the allure of transforming one's life through astute investments and a deep understanding of the financial markets. This book serves as a beacon for those yearning to break free from the conventional shackles of day jobs by harnessing the power and flexibility of options trading.

The author meticulously unveils the intricacies of options trading, shedding light on strategies that have stood the test of time. What makes this guide exceptional is its seamless blend of technical prowess with a profound emphasis on financial wisdom and the art of risk management. The narrative is clear: success in trading extends beyond mere transactions; it's about making informed, strategic decisions with a vision for enduring wealth and stability.

At its core, the book is a repository of knowledge, brimming with actionable insights, real-life scenarios, and step-by-step methodologies that empower even the novice trader to navigate the options market with confidence. The emphasis on cultivating a trader's mindset—marked by discipline, resilience, and an insatiable quest for learning— is a golden thread that runs through each chapter.

For individuals poised on the cusp of financial transformation, eager to decode the dynamism of options trading, "Escape the 9-to-5" offers more than strategies; it offers a new perspective on life and finance. It's an invitation to embark on a journey of personal and financial growth, where smart investing is the key to unlocking a world of possibilities.

Dive into "Escape the 9-to-5: Build Your Fortune with Proven Options Trading Strategies" and discover how the world of options trading can be your gateway to a life of financial autonomy and prosperity. Your journey towards escaping the mundane and embracing financial liberation begins with a simple click: https://a.co/d/2yorO5Q. Explore the book on Amazon and take the first step towards transforming your financial destiny.

Discover More from Ernie Braveboy

Embark on a journey of financial empowerment and trading mastery by exploring other insightful works by Ernie Braveboy. From comprehensive guides on trading strategies to deep dives into investment wisdom, each book offers valuable knowledge to enhance your financial acumen. Visit Ernie Braveboy's author page to uncover a treasure trove of resources tailored for your financial success.